Reviews & Endorsements:

"This work is an anointed blend of calling and passion, resulting in a spiritual masterpiece that encourages believers and inspires the lost."
-Womanstorm
spoken word artist & host - Durham, NC

"... an awesome ministry tool! The authors speak to so many people's situations and problems; I can see why this is titled 'Solace.' It's like a contemporary companion to the Word..."
-Derome Scott Smith, director
Living Word Stage Company - Richmond, VA

"The authors teach us as well as lead us. 'Going Through,' 'The Tale of Many Men,' 'Sometimes We Fall,' 'It Shall Come to Pass,' 'Genocide,' and 'Experience' have been birthed from deep introspection so that the verses don't preach—they share the process by which one acquires wisdom and understanding."
-Aisha R. Brantley, poet & author of <u>The Anointed Right Hand</u>
Baltimore, MD

"Éric & Will have masterfully combined their poetic gifts to present a spiritual tool; created to enlighten, encourage, and empower all who need solace in their lives. A job well done!"
-Elder Joe Howard, president & CEO
Strategic Solutions - Woodbridge, VA

"<u>Seeking Solace</u> contains bottom-line points on everyday life, packed with purpose and explorations of thoughts."
-SurAyah, poet and author of <u>Memoirs on Love and Life</u>
Washington, DC

"... truly a blessing. God must have had you send this to me right on time. I just finished crying about some deeply personal issues. And you are right, even poetry is 'Not Like A Prayer.' Praise God!!!"
-Tyesha Rice, student
Columbia Theological Seminary - Decatur, GA

"Oftentimes when I go through a situation, your poems enlighten me. I thank God for inspiring and using you to write because through your poetry lives are touched."

-*Sherry Harper - Virginia Beach, VA*
reader of E&W Collaborations

"The writings in this book are more than poetry. They are words to inspire the soul, lift the spirit, and recognize who we are and whom's we are. You will find yourself in solace when you live these words. Eric and Will will inspire you to become who God has declared you to be."

-*Pastor Ron Jones*
Agape Fellowship - Gricignano, Italy

"... my personal favorites... are '*Mr. Suicide Bomber...*' and '*I'm Maintaining...*' - Will and Éric definitely step up to the challenge of bringing light in the darkness, and hope in the midst of hopeless situations. It is truly a work of inspiration at a time when the world is desperate for healing."

-*Sonstar Carlisle Peterson, author of* <u>*The Destiny of the Black Race*</u>
apostle & founder of Nation Within A Nation Enterprises

"Eric & Will have captured a unique flavor of God's essence and have wrapped it into words of inspiration that cause provoking thoughts of inner peace. '*Blessed Assurance*' is a short, simple yet assuring word of comfort crafted in such a way that even the young may take comfort in."

-*Levonzia Stevens, Sr., author & senior pastor*
Hope Aglow Christian Center - Woodbridge, VA

"Wow, I really love this poem ('*Not Like A Prayer*'). It says so much about the true purpose of prayer and is very clearly written for understanding."

-*Tracee Jackson, Heart Tones Inspirational Company - Dallas, TX*

Other Books by Éric L Farrell:

Verbalizions of Enlightenment: The Secret to the Pain

SEEKING

SOLACE

Finding Peace and Comfort
in Times of Distress

May the Lord Bless and keep you in all things Phil 4:6-9

12/21/03

*To Hawk
May you find peace and comfort
in between the pages of this
book.*

Will

12/21/03

Éric L
Farrell

Will
Holmes Jr.

Emaculate Publishing

Published by:

Emaculate Publishing
P.O. Box 1074
Woodbridge, VA 22195

http://www.emaculatepublishing.com
info@emaculatepublishing.com
SAN: 254-2005

Library of Congress Control Number: 2003108942

Farrell, Eric L.
    Seeking solace: in a time of distress/ Eric L Farrell, Will Holmes Jr..
    p. cm.
ISBN: 1-931855-33-1 (hardcover)

1. Inspiration.   2. Poetry.   3. Self Help.
    4. African American Authors.   5. Christian Living.   6. Motivation.

                                                    2003108942

Cover art and design by Éric L Farrell of 4L Artistry
Edited by Jason L. Johnson

Printed in Canada
First printing

Blessed are they that mourn;
for they shall be comforted.

Blessed are the peacemakers:
for they shall be called the children of God.

-Matthew 5:4,9

CONTENTS

CONTENTS

(...continued)

Behind the Poems
(more about the topics, where the poems came from, relevant scriptures)

About the Authors

Dedication

Will:

> This book is dedicated to my parents, William Sr. and Helen. "Train up a child in the way he should go: and when he is old, he will not depart from it" (Proverbs 22:6). My parents provided me with the spiritual foundation and values I needed to be able to develop my relationship with Christ as I became older. Mom and Dad, thanks for placing in me the ability to seek the Lord at all times.

Éric:

> This book is dedicated to my mother, Hazel. Ma, thanks for allowing me to meet the world with all its harsh realities, while being there to nurture and provide me with solace when I found out that life was not fair and the world didn't really care. Thanks also for believing and being supportive as I stepped out on faith, deciding to dedicate all of my time and energy to reaching the world through books and poetry. This wouldn't be without you.

E&W Collaborations (Éric & Will):

> Together, we dedicate this book to Sonstar. Through him and his family, Christ has manifested a true example of resilience after losing a loved one. Soon after writing the foreword (and first poem) of this book, his beloved wife, Sandile, has faced an unexpected and sudden death, but only to live forever with the Lord above. Sonstar, thanks for allowing the most unpleasant experience in your life to be shared with the world, as you are a witness that Christ does provide solace in even the worst of situations.

Will's Acknowledgments

First, I would like to give honor and thanks to my **Lord** and Saviour Jesus Christ - without Him, neither my poetry nor this book would be possible. Again, thank you Lord for blessing me with this gift and allowing me to use it to encourage and uplift your people.

You know I have to give a big thank you to my **poetical partner** Éric L Farrell. E, thanks for helping me to realize my poetic talent and for motivating me (spiritually and generally) by showing me a model of hard work, dedication and perseverance. I would like to acknowledge and thank my **parents,** William, Sr. and Helen - thank you for always being there for me with wisdom, knowledge, and love;

I'm honored to acknowledge my **fiancée,** Bernell Turner (Berdie) – thanks for being there to help me regain my motivation and purpose for this book, for being accepting of the time that I had to put into it, and for your honest criticism while still being my number one fan;

My **brothers**, Mark and Allen, and my **sister**, Traci, for handing down "advice by experience," and helping me to avoid the harmful situations and opportunities, while taking advantage of the helpful situations and opportunities that life presented; my brother-in-law Jonathan and my sister-in-law Marella for supporting and encouraging me as if I was their biological brother;

I want to thank several **close friends** who were instrumental in their audience participation, support, encouragement, motivation, help, spiritual guidance and upliftment, and constant positive feedback when it was most needed; A big thank you to my **Pastor, Rev. Simeon Spencer and my home church** family at Union Baptist Church in Trenton, NJ, for providing a home to my spiritual foundation; And also Elder Joe Howard at New Life Anointed Ministries in Woodbridge, VA, who brought me to tears with his prophetic vision of the calling that God had on my life - Thanks for insipiring me to reach this level of boldness and ministry.

I also would like to thank the many **other family** members, friends, and co-workers that are an important part of my life, but that I didn't have space to mention - Thank you for the support and motivation you provided for me at one time or another - whether it was being a faithful E&W e-mail **reader** or audience listener, giving compliments on my work, or unknowingly being the inspiration for some of my poems.

Eric's Acknowledgments

First and foremost, I thank you **Lord** and Saviour, Jesus Christ, for valuing me and providing necessary opportunities, replacing thin air with solid ground whenever I've stepped out on faith, and for providing me with the Comfort of the Holy Spirit as you inspired me to live, and love my work, and help others to do the same.

My **readers, poets,** and WordStage poetry people (including Traci Culver and the Barnes & Noble staff), for your love, feedback, inspiration, and the help many of you have gone out of your way to give;

My **family** that has grown with me: Will Holmes Jr., for working with me in E&W and other areas in life, being a spiritual partner, remaining forward and honest, yet willing to end disagreements without argument; my mother, Hazel, for your guidance and instruction; my dad, Calvin, for your faith in God, growing humbleness and for allowing me to grow and again getting to know, love, and respect me as a man of my own; my brother, Calvin and his wife, Liz, for keeping your heart open with love and encouragement; my grandparents, Ethel, Helen, Elsie, Vernie and Herbert "The Forerunner," for laying a foundation of faith; my aunts, uncles, and cousins, for your love; my nephew Ajala, for the watchful and patient spirit you exhibited while coming to understanding (truly a noble way we learn from a newborn); Sazara, for opening your heart, believing in me, uplifting and supporting me, and being a spiritual partner...

My **spiritual leaders in Christ** previously acknowledged, along with Pastor Lance Watson, for the poetic opportunity, also for denying the flesh to maintain Spiritual connection (evidenced in your messages); Pastor Jonah Obonyo, for your humble spirit and hospitality; and my New Life Africa Team, for providing spiritual support, your lean-on-shoulder, and obedient heart; my New Life and St. Paul's family for the love; Rory Lyon and all my brothers and sisters in Christ, for truly being family wherever I travel;

The first **Authors** introducing themselves into my life, for providing feedback, encouragement and inspiration: Duane G. Foster "The Blacksheep," for walking with me in this "outcastic" poetic calling of Truth; E. Ethelbert Miller, for your time and advisement in this process; Michael Eric Dyson, for my MLK book gift; Michael Moore and Sonia Sanchez, for doing more than your part in taking a stand for authors' freedom of speech; Linda Pastan, for your inspiring personal endorsement of my first book; Ruth N. Segres, April Barrett, Sharon Johnson, Aisha Brantley, and Collage, for standing with me in this poetic conquest against Death; Dana Hawes, for introducing me to the poetry lounge scene;Thanx all!

E&W 's Acknowledgments

We would like to thank a few people who have played important roles in our lives and our E&W Collaborations ministry.

We'd like to thank our Lord and Saviour, Jesus Christ, for keeping E&W going and making sure our poems were relevant to what people needed to hear.

We'd like to thank Shelton Gregory, for volunteering and publishing our first website before we ever thought of it; Mrs. Emily Ware, for holding us to higher writing standards when we wanted to take the easy way out of your Honors English class; Jason L. Johnson "The English Genius," for being a big brother, scholarly role-model, and an amazing editor for this book project (we'll nominate you for the Golden Red Pen Award); Apostle Sonstar Peterson, for being a man of humbleness and dedication to Truth, excellence and refinement, and for reviewing this book and dedicating yourself to help fulfill the purpose of this ministry... "The world waits to hear what you've learned from it"; Andrew Rogers, for being there for us, an example of humility, honesty, and loyalty; Daryl Barkley "The Ginger-bread Man" (catch him if you can), for being a big brother to us as we learned about life through collegiate eyes; Dondrae Maiden, for providing us (as freshmen) with an example of a man of God who doesn't forsake his morals for popular trends once leaving home, also for being an example of dedication and perseverance; Robert Youngblood "The Motivator," for motivating us and never expecting anything less than better from us, also for being an example of undying determination; Kelly Carter, for never forgetting us - we'll never forget you; Nah-Deh Simmons "Noodles," for keeping us on our toes by always presenting us with another viewpoint... you're right, nobody can beat you - if God is for you, who can be against you?; David Bailey and the Alive in Christ family 2001, for being true examples of brothers and sisters in Christ and hosting us on our first performance as "E&W Collaborations"; Kindra Leeper, for being a faithful reader and sending us all of the lost E&W poems when Hotmail wiped out the contents of our email account; all of our readers, for encouraging us with your replies and forwarding our poetry to the world, also for requesting that we write a book (here it is); all of our fam' from Virginia Union University, for providing us with the learning experiences from which we write... Four years later, E&W still exists because of all of you. Thank You!

Thanks be to the Lord above!

Foreword

Inspiration Kept You Sane

by Sonstar Carlisle Peterson

Inspiration is the breath of God,
Giving life to all living.
A soul once dead, now erupts in thanksgiving.
Inspiration is the gift of God,
Tapping springs of creativity.
Innovation in your soul takes flight,
You were predestined from your nativity.
Inspiration is the power of God,
You'll transcend the insanity.
As the eagle flies to kiss the sun,
Above the storms and calamity... And yet, and yet!
A baby cries, a mother dies, a brother stops to question why,
This tragedy you can't deny.
The pain inside your heart's no lie.
Now all you want to do is cry... no, there's more,
Truth is, you really want to die... but then, but then!
A window opens and light shines in,
Soothing your soul, compassionate friend.
You know, though you sit, hand tucked under your chin,
You can't quit, it's not the end; in fact, it's your time to begin.
While the world waits to hear what you've learned from it;
Yes they wait... they know that you've earned from it.
God made the mountains, majestic in their ranges
That you may climb over, not bow to worship them,
Whilst going through the changes.
What's really not strange is,
Through the dark night of your pain, you made it through the rain
Inspiration kept you sane.

July 2003

I love the words, creativity, innovation, inventiveness and inspiration of this book. The words and the thought of their meaning do something special to the depth of my being. Having spent many years in the entertainment world, I came to understand the value of inspiration in the lives of people as they go through their daily routines. The arts shape our culture and impact upon our thinking for good or for evil.

After many years of being distinguished as a dancer, choreographer, singer and songwriter, I realized that songs are poetic. Still, I had never tried my hand at poetry as a distinct art form for many years. Once I did, I experienced a level of individual expression that I had never touched before in songwriting.

When I read Éric L Farrell's first book release, *Verbalizions of Enlightenment: The Secret to the Pain*, I was hooked from the first poem, *"Verbalizions."* I immediately felt his individual soul and uniqueness of expression. It was not hard to see why a poem written by him (*"They Follow You Follow Them"*), could emerge as the top pick of many poems submitted to the Russell Simmons *Def Poetry Jam* in September 2001.

This new work by Éric L Farrell and Will Holmes Jr. is, without a doubt, a living testament to the power of synergy in poetry. It is aptly titled *"Seeking Solace: Finding Peace and Comfort in Times Of Distress."* The word "solace" means, comfort in sorrow or misfortune or trouble; alleviation of distress or discomfort.... The world does not need more people who use the creative arts to promote everything from licentiousness to utter depravity. It needs people whose works of art can inspire and bring hope in the midst of a world filled with darkness and hopelessness.

Will and Éric definitely step up to the challenge of bringing light in the darkness, and hope in the midst of hopeless situations. It is truly a work of inspiration at a time when the world is desperate for healing.

I'm sure that as this work is shared, it will touch many deep areas in the souls of those who read it, based on the experiences they will identify with. They will come away with the reflections, meditations, cogitations and deliberations that improve our situations through the light of inspirations. I encourage all who read it to share it with your friends, so they too can find solace. My personal favorites from the two authors are *"Mr. Suicide Bomber"* by Éric L Farrell and *"I'm Maintaining"* by Will Holmes Jr.

Sonstar Carlisle Peterson
Apostle & Founder of Nation Within A Nation Enterprises
Author of <u>*The Destiny of the Black Race*</u>

I Write This Song For You
(from Sonstar 10/19/2003)

Sandile*
Did I see your face, in some far away place?
Seems like I knew you long before we met
Girl I liked your style
I was captured by your smile
From that day I knew I never could forget, you
I wanted you for my wife
I was prepared to spend my life, with you
And though sometimes it has been bitter sweet
The Jesus in you girl has made my life complete

I write this song for you
A token of my love for all you've helped me through
I write this song for you
A tribute to your love because you've always been true
I write this song for you
The warm fire of your love always made me feel brand new
I write this song for you
You've been my queen, I take this time to say how much
you've meant to me
Cause you inspired me

I remember when, times were so discouraging
Seemed like I'd never see the light of day
But then there you came, in your own familiar way
Through your faith you helped me stand to call the play
Through your eyes I came to see
Depths and dimensions of what love could be
As we walked in the light of truth's transparency
And touched what could only be experienced unselfishly
Only God could make two people fit so perfectly

*Sandile -pronounced san-dee-lee   ...poem continued>

But when I woke in the morning you were gone
You took your flight transcending earth's battle zone
You've graduated the struggle, taking your place before the throne
I know you never planned to leave me here alone
To walk through a process I had never known
Without my twin, flesh of my flesh and bone of my bone
How do I say goodbye to my friend?
I'll not say goodbye, only, "until we meet again"
It's not a question of if, only a matter of when
Although I miss you here, I'm so glad you're there, with Him
Baby doll you are so unique, even more so now dwelling in unapproachable light
You'll never again have to walk through the perils of night
I will always love you Sandile
You'll never be in my past, I see you in my future

Seven Sent

Seven poems sent by Éric L Farrell
Seven poems sent by Will Holmes Jr.

I've written and sent these seven poems by e-mail to tell **the tale of many men**. *Sometimes we fall*, but while *going through*, we gain **experience.** Even when it seems like there is **no escape, *I'm maintaining***. When **losing a loved one**, I've questioned: "Is this a **fair life?**" Yet, I must remain focused and **fear less**, knowing that **it shall come to pass**. So **mr. suicide bomber**, you may try to initiate **genocide**, causing me to question: "**Lord, why?**" You may try to gain solace with your vengeance, and I may try to gain solace with revenge, but even the most vengeful plans are **not like a prayer**.

The Tale of Many Men [Introduction]

Have you ever forgotten your purpose in life or felt dead on the inside?

I'm sure you have. This poem is for ALL of us because everybody has felt this way at some time, and we have all sinned and fallen short of God's Glory (Romans 3:23). The difference is whether we say "oh well" and keep doing it, or if we acknowledge our problem, apologize to God, and ask for His help to strengthen us enough to overcome it. We can overcome anything.

The Tale of Many Men

The Lord is my Saviour
With the Lord I found favor
Without the Lord, i'm Kool-Aid with no flavor

He guided my path
With the rod and the staff
Without the Lord, I wouldn't even have half

I can only be real
He discarded my mask
The Lord then washed me up
With the Holiest bath

I then felt His presence
And mine too, at last!
And only then, could I begin to grow like green grass

The temple of my body had been torn down
By the Devil's wrecking crew
I was strapped to the ground

Are you listening to me?
I know how this sounds
You're probably taking this lightly or giving me frowns

To hear Satan's name, is not an everyday thing
But you deal with him daily
He just never looks the same

...poem continued>

You've met him many times under alias names
But this time, he *will* be catching the blame

Who do you think that was that bumped you the other day?
Did you recognize those eyes that looked at you in a
    funny way?
Have you ever asked yourself, "How could I do such a thing?"
And then avoid the mirror, so you wouldn't deal with guilt
    and shame?

You can say what you want
But I've played that game
And repented repeatedly, but still did the same thing

And repented repeatedly, but still did the same thing

And repented repeatedly, but still did the same thing

It's a spiritual battle
No man wins alone
We're prodigal children
And we need to come home

Somebody asked the Lord to come to my aid
I just know in my heart that somebody prayed
The gleam in my eyes had started to fade
The pep in my step was somewhat delayed
My energy was like solar power in shade
My strength was that of a newborn babe
My nerves were shaky and tattered and frayed
My prayers got repetitive and had become vague

My faith was dying; my hope was decayed
My heart was callous like I'd been betrayed
But just before my last note had been played
I was brought to my senses by Jesus who stayed
I wondered astray, but Jesus had stayed

Jesus stayed

And even though the Lord carried me, I had to move first
And turn to Him when I realized it would only get worse

And I was so relieved to return home from dark
   adventures of sin

And this same,
Has been the story and the tale of many men.

7/9/00
-Éric L Farrell

Sometimes We Fall *[Introduction]*

You're sleeping GOOD. The alarm clock goes off... what do you do?

If you're like me, you *hit the Snooze button* for ten more minutes of sleep. Now relate that to your life and your Christian walk.

Many times we're in situations that aren't healthy for our mind, body, or spirit. Maybe we're involved in unhealthy relationships. Maybe we have bad habits that we can't seem to break. Maybe we're involved with people or activities that aren't positively affecting our lives. When family and close friends offer advice, we think they don't understand, but *we* may be the ones who don't see what's going on. So do we listen? Nope... we just *hit the Snooze button* and stay asleep, not wanting to wake up to see the truth.

We decide to enjoy a few more moments in the darkness, until we realize that the extra Snooze time isn't really helping us feel better. It just makes us late. When we finally wake up, we're usually too late to meet our appointment... and there's no getting that time back.

Don't miss your appointments with God!

Sometimes We Fall...

Sometimes we fall off,
Sometimes we step back.
But we can't just give up
We gotta get back on track.

Sometimes we leave,
We may stray away,
But we can always come back,
Just ask to be shown the way.

Sometimes we want to close our ears to the truth,
For the fear that we may hear it.
Yeah, everybody knows it's hard to sleep with a convicted
  spirit.

Sometimes we can't see what is right,
We become blinded.
But if we TRULY search for the light,
Trusting Him, we can find it.

Many of us want the pleasures of life now,
And say we'll live right later.

I know you may be young,
And I'm not trying to be a party-hater,
But more sooner than later,
You'll fall out of God's grace,
And won't enjoy His Divine favor.

...poem continued>

Sometimes sin has us under control.
We take pleasure in it at the time,
But it takes its toll...

Take this message in as a whole.
We may enjoy sinful, worldly ways now,
But we're damaging our soul!

Sometimes in our Christian walk,
We do more sleep-walking than righteous walking.
When talking, we share more gossip
And do more fussin' and cussin'
Than we do spending time having Christian discussion.

Yeah, sometimes we slip,
We all make mistakes...
But it's all about the moves we make...
Which path *we decide* to take.

Sometimes we fall down,
But we gotta get back up.
Yeah, it's hard and it's tough;
But with God's help, the storm will end,
And we'll earn back His love and His trust.
If that Christian spirit inside us is sleep,
It's time to WAKE UP!

4/16/01
-Will Holmes Jr.

Going Through [Introduction]

Why do we go through such rough times in life?

We've heard that "God works in mysterious ways," but what does this really mean?

God works everything out in order to accomplish His will, and there are so many factors that affect our lives that we can't see how they will all work together. So we call them mysterious since we don't fully understand how God uses them to accomplish His will. I'm glad we're not required to understand.

What is God's will?

God wants all things to work out in a way that will benefit those who love Him and can help fulfill His purpose. It's that simple. (Ephesians 1:9-11; Romans 8:28)

How does God accomplish His will?

He gives each of our lives a specific purpose, which ultimately benefits all of us who love Him. However, sometimes while remaining in God's will, we go through hardships. We don't always know why we must endure them, but we're comforted by knowing that our situation is only temporary and that God knows what He's doing.

To accomplish His will, God has ways and means that are often unknown to man (mysterious). So we place our faith in God, knowing that He's using every pleasant and unpleasant circumstance in His plan to permanently bless us so much, that we'll forget all past troubles. (2 Corinthians 4:17)

God's will is simple: to benefit us. He's much better at doing this than we are, so He does all the work. This way, we can't lose!

Going Through

Some people often question why we go through...
Trivial travails, like swimming in glue

Longsuffering ain't ever been a short term thing
We want to eat from God's table, but what do we bring?

The song we most sing, is nothing more than half done
If you see the moon shine, then expect the sun

If the first verse sung wasn't nothing but trouble
Then pretty soon God gon' have the pleasure to double

If the first verse of life was all Godless fun
Then the last verse of life will probably make you run

That's the way that it is and that's the way that it's done
With the God Almighty and His Holy Son

If you want to change the rules, then you take it to Him
If you need to change your life, then it's time to begin

'Cause all things work together for the good of those
Who love the Lord and have Heavenly goals

Yet, I'm so often tempted to question God
But the answers to life could make life more hard

Patience is a virtue that we often lack
When we forget that God knows when to hold us back

Sending distractions that frustrate us
So we get upset with Him, not knowing He just saved us...

Some time, some heartache, or maybe our life
Is what we have to thank Him for in our time of strife.

5/20/00
-Éric L Farrell

Experience [Introduction]

How have your experiences changed your life?

This poem challenges us to evaluate what we've been through, what we're going through, what we may face in the future, and the impact of these experiences.

Experience

You may recognize your best experience as your worst...

Let this submerse...

Now hear this vice verse...

What you claim as your best experience yet,
may have been your downfall

Let US not forget.

———————————

10/24/99
-Éric L Farrell-

No Escape [Introduction]

Do you feel trapped in a situation?

Does it seem like no matter what you do, nothing seems to make it better? Have you tried to follow God's voice, but still fulfill your own desires instead of His desires? Maybe you've gotten into a bad situation that seems like it will never end. Well, this poem is for you. Remember one thing – many times in life, we go through trials and tribulations that help to prepare us for a greater blessing. You may not be able to *see* the light at the end of your tunnel, but trust in the Lord to guide you through the darkness. You shouldn't feel like you have no escape, because with faith in Him, you will always reach the light at the end.

No Escape

Are you in a situation, with no way out?
Different paths to choose, but each was the wrong route?
Took the way you thought best,
Still caught in the trap, failed your quest.
You chose the way you thought was right,
But was it really right...?
Or did you force it into God's will
By the justification of your own might?

Are you stuck in a situation, real-life catch 22?
Damned if you don't, damned if you do...
Your light is dim and your spirit is blue.
Instead of heeding God's voice,
You decided your OWN will and desires to be true.

Falling short of His glory,
And out of His grace,
Backing up a couple steps,
Instead of running the good race.

Feeling trapped in the mess,
Starting to lose hope,
Losing touch with the real world,
Irritability and stress don't help you cope.

But you've got to move on,
Although the road is long,
Keep pushing with all your might...
'Cause once the storm is over,
The sun will shine bright.

...poem continued>

Remember,
God will never put more on you than you can bear,
Take your worries to Him,
And His comforting touch, He will share.

We go through trials and tribulations,
They help us to grow...
We go through unimaginable situations,
They teach us lessons we need to know.

It's said that for every dark cloud there's a silver lining...
Well, I say: *For every dark situation...*
You have to find where God's light is shining.

If you still wonder why things happen the way they do...
Then listen and take notes
I've got The *Good News* for you:

God's ways are greater, and His thoughts are higher,
Life is about living for Him,
Not for your own desire.
The quicker you learn, the better off you'll be,
And once you learn the lesson He wants you to see,
All that you could ever want and need...
He shall give it to thee.

1/16/02
-Will Holmes Jr.

I'm Maintaining [Introduction]

Sometimes life is hard - real hard.

We sometimes find it difficult to make it through the hour, the day, or the rest of the week. We can easily get down, depressed, and distressed over the problems and situations we go through. But how do we maintain? Well, the answer is at the end of this poem (don't peek)…

I'm Maintaining

Mentally draining,
Money is straining,
Mom's complaining...
-But... I'm Maintaining-

Times are rough,
Hard to cope,
Make me wanna tie the knot,
Hang from the rope...
-Instead... I'm Maintaining-

Fam' is dying,
Kids are crying,
My lady is lying,
Tired of trying,
How'd I get fired before applying?!
-How am I doing?... Maintaining-

Head under water,
Turn tricks for quarters,
Got nobody supportive...
-Still... Maintaining-

Surrounded by thugs,
Great minds on drugs,
I gets no love, no hugs,
Ready to bug,
My grave already dug.
I can't believe it...
-I'm Still Maintaining-

Feeling the pain,
Dumb in my brain.
Feeling hate from my brothers,
Like Abel did Cain.
Going insane,
Wanna jump in front of the train!
-But somehow... I Maintain-

Hunger inside,
Losing my pride,
Nobody on my side,
No confidence to ride...
-Hmm... Still I Maintain-

Haters are hunting
Talent is nothing
Fakes are fronting
Forget 'em all. Bump 'em!
-But... Why am I Maintaining?-

Well, I'll tell ya the deal...
Open your heart,
'Cause Jesus Christ is real.

If you're hurting,
Got a big burden...
Give it to Him.
You get the point, I don't gotta explain.
Learn real peace,
Troubles will cease, and you'll Maintain

...poem continued>

So, stay in the chase, run the good race;
And continue to maintain...
MAINTAIN YOUR FAITH.

7/8/99
-Will Holmes Jr.

Losing A Loved One [Introduction]

Sometimes it's hard when we lose someone close to us, especially if it happens suddenly and tragically.

I went through the loss of my Aunt and Uncle (my Dad's sister and brother) around Thanksgiving and Christmas of 1998. They were in a car accident. My Aunt died by the time she got to the hospital, and my Uncle passed away the following month, right before Christmas. The words of this poem were comforting to me, and I pray it will help someone else deal with the loss of a loved one...

Losing A Loved One

It hurts when people we love turn into people we lose,
Taken so suddenly, without any clues.

Think back and be thankful,
Keep the good memories in mind.
You had the chance to share with that loved one,
God blessed you with that time.

Emotions are hard to suppress,
So if you want, let the tears flow.
But if you remember the good times,
Only your smiles will show.

11/25/98
-Will Holmes Jr.

Fair Life? [Introduction]

Does life always go exactly the way we'd like it to go?

No. Life never goes exactly the way we'd like it to go. We say that our life isn't fair. However, sometimes what seems to be unfair, is actually for our best. Everything in our lives will not always be pleasant. If it were, then we would never learn how to depend on our Heavenly Father for comfort, direction, and help.

Fair Life?

Sometimes we don't always get what we want.
Look, I'm gonna keep it real with you,
Make it blunt.
Life ain't fair, don't think different.
Not everybody cares, no matter how hard you wish it.
But remember, behind every dark cloud is a brighter day,
So stay optimistic, keep hope and pray.
And when things don't go your way...
Wasn't meant to be, don't stress,
You'll have your day.

It may look bad, but you never know God's plans,
Best thing you can do is not worry,
Leave it in His hands.
Be thankful for what's going right, no matter how little,
And don't try to guess why certain things happen,
You may not ever solve life's riddle.

Only God knows the whole plan, so just follow His lead,
Let Him work everything out for you,
And you shall succeed.

3/3/98
-Will Holmes Jr.

Fear Less [Introduction]

"Don't be scurred!" Fear less...

We've experienced many instances of terrorizing acts throughout the last few years. We've had terrorists, serial killers, anthrax, and school shootings. In Northern VA, we've even had a serial flasher breaking into people's homes armed with bare skin. Yes, you read it right, a serial flasher (a sick world huh?). With all of these sick people in the world, we need to remain watchful and cautious as we go about our normal lives; but fear not. Yes, these people may affect our lives in some way, BUT through our relationship with Christ, we can positively affect their lives in a much greater way. We have no reason to be afraid of anything or anybody when we walk with Jesus.

You've already come into contact with people who are possessed, if it's not you, yourself. Forget what you may have seen on <u>The Exorcist</u>; instead, look at the possessed people you're warned about on the evening news. No, their heads aren't spinning around on their necks, but nevertheless, they're possessed. They don't even know themselves and they can't explain why they do the things they do. Would Jesus be afraid of these people? Of course not; He'd try to save them and I'm sure He'd succeed. So why should we be afraid if we have the power, love, and soundness of mind that Christ had? I know we can't just flip a switch to turn off our fear, but the more and more we follow and trust God, the more our courage and strength will grow. Regardless of what you may believe, you can live a completely fearless life. Many of your brothers and sisters in Christ are already doing it, including myself. We're not pretending to be fearless because we think that's the Godly thing to do. We just don't see the need to be afraid. Why should we fear anything if we've got the Almighty God on our side?

Fear Less

Do you know what fearless means?
Have you ever had that feeling?
Have you ever walked down the street
Not giving a care about who's killing?

When my number is called
I'll be ready and more than willing
Because the only one who knows it
Can do miracles through healing

People harder than me
Have more fear in their eye
Because they don't really know
Where they're going when they die

To tell you the truth
I ain't even gon' lie
There's nothing I can do
If it's me you want to try

You can take what you want
I'm still gonna breathe
If you want to take that
You better hurry up and leave

For what I am
The spirit of fear is not in me
It's a fact not to test
Psalm twenty-seven: three

Some believe eye
Is a window to the soul
Believe it or not
With the red I roll

Red eye signifies
The burning of the soul
I don't care what you read
Or even what you were told

Some eyes burn
With wrath against Hell
Some foretell
That that's where they'll dwell

Fearless...
That man who's brave to rebel
Against ALL evil
And live to retell.

Are you?

5/13/98
-Éric L Farrell

It Shall Come to Pass [Introduction]

When we're in the midst of certain situations in life, we sometimes find ourselves questioning God.

We question, "*Why* is this happening to me? *When* will this problem go away?" We may even question whether God is truly paying us any attention. Even when we pray and praise God while enduring, we may still question Him if we don't *see* a change. Well, a change is on the way. I can testify from my own experiences that the change will be right on time. Sometimes God does not work how or as soon as we expect Him to work, but if we wait a little longer, we'll see that "*It Shall Come To Pass*," just as He promised.

It Shall Come to Pass

I'm lost in this world,
Don't know which way to turn.
I think I go right,
But a hard lesson is all I learn.
I've lost my direction; don't know what step to take...
I believe failure is my ultimate fate.

REMEMBER THE LESSON YOU LEARNED;
IT'S ALL PART OF THE PLAN.
FORGET FATE,
SUCCESS WILL COME, JUST FOLLOW THE LIGHT FROM
HEAVEN'S GATE.
ASK ME FOR GUIDANCE TO AVOID FAILURES PAST;
AND SUCCESS... IT SHALL COME TO PASS.

Lord, I've got problems and all I do is worry.
Nothing is going right,
And my vision of You is blurry.

READ MY WORD AND GLORIFY MY NAME;
PRAY AND KEEP FAITH ON THE PATH,
AND YOUR PHASE... IT SHALL COME TO PASS.

I've been misjudged.
Everywhere I look,
I get evil eyes, instead of supporting hugs.

I SHALL JUDGE THEM AS THEY HAVE JUDGED YOU,
AND IT SHALL COME TO PASS.

...poem continued>

My enemies surround me and continue to attack,
I tried to ignore, but I just gotta get revenge and fight back.

KEEP PEACE, NO WEAPON FORMED AGAINST YOU SHALL
   PROSPER.
I'LL MAKE THEM YOUR FOOTSTOOL TO STEP HIGHER.
THEY SHALL FEEL MY WRATH,
JUST STAY CALM, AND THIS TOO SHALL COME TO PASS.

I thought I had true friends,
But they turned around.
Now I'm *going through*, and they are nowhere to be found.

TRUE FRIENDS WITH TRUE SPIRIT,
I WILL PLACE IN YOUR PATH.
JUST DON'T YOU TURN AWAY FROM THEM,
AND IT SHALL COME TO PASS.

Lord, when will I find true love?
I've been hurt so many times,
I've even lost touch with your love from above.
I've given up on true love,
I no longer want someone else's hand to hold and rub.

JUST REMEMBER,
THE TRUE LOVE OF YOUR LIFE WILL BE YOUR LAST.
HAVE PATIENCE AND TRUST IN WHAT I WILL DO,
AND IT SHALL COME TO PASS.

Lord, I need money; I'm near broke...
And this situation I'm in, I feel my life going up in smoke...

Not to mention my family life has taken a turn for the worse,
We speak no more words of love,
We just curse.

TAKE COMFORT IN MY ROD AND MY STAFF,
I'LL TURN THAT ANGER INTO A LAUGH,
AND THIS TOO... SHALL COME TO PASS.

Lord, there's so many things I don't understand.
If I can't hear You when You answer my questions,
How can I follow Your plan?

KEEP STUDYING MY WORD,
AND PRAYING FOR THE ANSWERS YOU SEEK.
IF YOU TRUST THAT I WILL ANSWER ON TIME,
WISDOM AND UNDERSTANDING YOU SHALL REAP.
ALLOW YOUR FAITH TO RUN DEEP,
AND REMEMBER THAT I SAID, "IT SHALL COME TO PASS,"
FOR THAT IS A PROMISE I SHALL KEEP.

7/8/01
-Will Holmes Jr.

Mr. Suicide Bomber [Introduction]

Some people have killed themselves and others, thinking that such a deed would afford them the solace of Heaven.

This poem is a case of a man ready to go to such an extreme in search of God's loving arms. However, it becomes obvious that there are certain truths that he has overlooked. Perhaps he's been brought up in a society that neglected him of the true love and comfort that can be received by all of us from God Almighty. Maybe they didn't tell him that God's love and comfort are free gifts to us. Maybe he's been taught to believe that God's love is something that must be earned by a lifetime worth of deeds. Understand that people of this sort are often desperate to get out of their hurtful living conditions, and will do almost anything to get to a place where they can receive the comfort of God's love. Perhaps they're desperate enough that they may believe a man who tells them that God's love is only in Heaven. Thus, they may be persuaded to kill themselves or die fighting for "His cause" as an effort to receive this comforting love.

Make no mistake, suicide is not a way to Heaven; neither is genocide. And God's love exists on earth as well as in Heaven. We don't have to kill anyone to get it. We don't even have to earn it. We just have to accept it.

"FOR GOD SO LOVED THE WORLD, THAT HE GAVE HIS ONLY BEGOTTEN SON, THAT WHOSOEVER BELIEVETH IN HIM SHOULD NOT PERISH, BUT HAVE EVERLASTING LIFE."

-John 3:16

Mr. Suicide Bomber

Mr. Suicide Bomber,
How do you do?
I know you have something more important to do
But if I may just have the first minute of your time
It might be nice for us to share a piece of mind
You understand that later this will be impossible for us two
So let's make sure you've fully expressed yourself before
  it's all through
Ok, I'll try to understand the way you see this whole thing:
The people around us, me, you, and this bomb you bring
Which, by the way, looks kind of heavy
Your back must be strained!
So while we talk, you can put it over there on the ground
No, nobody will bother it
I'm sure they won't like the sound.

Ok now, I agree with you.
Some of these people ain't right!
Seems like some of these people need to die TONIGHT!
But truth be told, me and you have done bad things too
And if they're worthy of death, then we're worthy of it too
NO! NO! WAIT!   COME BACK!
That's not what I'm saying you need to do
I told you... just leave it over there until the conversation is
  through.
Now, back to what I was sayin'...
There's a flaw in the plan
Because the Devil wins a soul when you kill a sinful man
And with all these people in here... that's a bountiful supply
So how exactly does that benefit the Big Man in the Sky?

...poem continued>

I'm not saying it's the work of the Devil
I'm just saying it's on the same level
Because in terms of soul achievement, the Devil would
  definitely get the gold medal

So you say for this, YOU will get to go to Heaven?
If you'll send all these men to Hell...

No, I'm not saying your act is Hellish
But if I must say so myself, I'd say it sounds a bit selfish

I hear that salvation is something Allah doesn't assure
But for a lifetime it's something that must be worked toward
But if a Muslim dies in a "holy" war
Allah will fulfill his *only* promise of a heavenly reward
Hmm...

That sounds like something to consider, but let's look at
  the bigger picture
I mean, I'd think about joining you,
But let's ask ourselves some questions before we just go
  pull the trigger...
To me, it almost sounds too good to be true
For real... doesn't it sound too good to you?
Does the jihad promise still apply if you kill you?
There's another flaw in the plan
If you're righteous and you kill yourself, then you've just
  killed a righteous man
How can a dead man seek atonement (or forgiveness) for
  righteous blood on his hands?
Hmm...

Nevertheless,
Let's pretend that you'd still go to the heavenly sky
Some of these people in here don't deserve to die!

If you kill those righteous men, is that yet not a sin?
I mean, honestly, where does accountability begin?

If this death is so prestigious, then why didn't they send bin?
Does Allah's heavenly reward not apply to him?
So why did bin Laden run from death in the end?
Why do the leaders only prescribe death for common men?
Why don't they go speak to the masses like Martin Luther
  King Jr. and them?
King knew that someone wanted to put a bullet in him.

The truth is...

They care as much about you as those videotapes they send
You know they got another copy...

They got another man just like you
Who bin threw the same things that you been threw

Mr. Bomber Man, you don't have to pull out the pin
We love you Bomber Man
Don't die for deceitful men

We need a hero...

9/12/02
-Éric L Farrell

Genocide [Introduction]

The Tragedy of September 11ᵗʰ (9-11) is the introduction to this poem.

This poem was conceived in an attempt to verbalize the confused feelings that we've had in America since 9-11. It was born in an attempt to cause people to think logically about what's going on and how we're handling these types of occurrences. The mind frame that *The Attacks* have caused us to have is not far from the mind frame of one who later pleads "temporary insanity." Temporary insanity is a momentary condition where the person is unable to think logically about what they're doing, and take the wrong course of "corrective action." Well... by now, we've had plenty of time to think logically about our actions (and reactions). Yet, many of us haven't shown that we've given the situation any logical thought or spiritual consideration.

Many of us have claimed to walk by faith and not by sight, but as soon as something happens and we can't see why, we throw our faith out of the window and start making convenient assumptions. We make these assumptions because we want to convince ourselves that we have a reason to take up arms and fight. Our minds can't rest until we know the problem is resolved. However, the real problem is often our hastiness and lack of faith in God. With faith in God, we would know that their punishment is being handled by the Lord above.

Vengeance is a weapon that man will never learn how to use effectively, because vengeance is the Lord's.

Genocide

Genocide

Many a people lied
Many lied down and died
Many good people cried

Many people forgot their God-given title
Turning the other cheek got confused with being idle
Vengeance has become man's attempt toward revival
But instructions for it were too complex to be imbibled*

So now we're in confusion
Basing decisions on illusions
How can we be in control
When we can't see the fate we're choosing?

Many families will never forget the members that *ben* lost
So many will spend their lives, trying to bring 'em back
    at any cost
So many more will fall in the Fall when leaves' colors cross
So blood will season the ground like a condiment of sauce

We put the icing on the cake
Prepared for Revelational fate
How can we save a soul
Without a piece of peace on the plate?

Genocide

Many people alive
Don't know how they feel inside
Either compassion or pride

*imbibled - written in the Bible   *...poem continued>*

Many fall in condemNation from Genesis to Revelation
They put words in God's mouth about how to deal with the
  situation
When the Lord returns, the militaries will man their station
They do these things because they lack spiritual realization

We haven't kept our faith in God
So we get mad at the firing squad
How can we blame them
When we barely even do our job?

Many people have not enrolled in futury class
So many still don't know the future was written in the past
Genocide becomes suicide because man kills mankind at last
They may be in another land, but they are still on the
  same path

We're under the same sky
We all come from the same Guy
How can we go see Heaven
With a grudge and a hostile eye?

Genocide

Many can't coincide
So God won't let them inside
Where peaceful people reside

...For-givin

10/08/01
-Éric L Farrell

Lord, Why? [Introduction]

Tuesday, September 11, 2001 is a day that will never be forgotten.

The heartfelt thoughts and prayers of E&W went out to those directly affected by this tragedy and to the country as a whole. Our prayers also went out to those who initiated this event, because God teaches us to forgive, love, and pray for our enemies and that He'll use them as our footstool. Most people have voiced their opinion about this tragedy, and responded with the action they thought should be taken. This poem is my response.

"Lord, Why?" reflects a question-answer session with God.

Lord, Why?

Where do I go now?
Which way do I turn?
Many things I don't understand,
And so much more to learn.

SEEK AND YE SHALL FIND,
ASK AND IT SHALL BE GIVEN,
BUT AT THE RIGHT TIME.

But Lord, why are things the way they are?
Why, at times, does it seem You aren't near, but far?
Why do You let this happen...or that?
My life is in shambles, so where are You at?

MY CHILD, I'VE NEVER LEFT YOU, YOU JUST LOST FAITH.
MANY HARSH THINGS ARE NOT MY PURPOSE OR ABSENCE
  OF ME,
THEY ARE THE PRESENCE OF EVIL AND HATE.
I KNOW MY WILL IS HARD TO FOLLOW,
AND EVERYTHING THAT HAPPENS IS SOMETIMES HARD TO
  SWALLOW.
BUT MY THOUGHTS AND WAYS ARE GREATER THAN YOURS,
SO DON'T LOSE YOUR TRUST.
LIVE FOR ME AND I'll WATCH OVER YOU, THAT'S A PROMISE
BETWEEN US.

Lord, when I think back, I now understand.
I did stop reading my Bible as much,
So I guess I lost touch with Your hand.

And my prayer life slowed down,
To the point my soul was in danger.
I stopped talking to You,
Maybe that's why You seemed like a stranger.

I won't question You Lord,
I will continue to praise You and stay in Your Will,
Through success and trials, knowing You are with me still.

WISDOM YOU ARE BEGINNING TO GAIN.
NEVER HESITATE TO CALL ON MY NAME.
I'M YOUR COMFORTER, YOUR SAVIOUR, YOUR PROVIDER,
YOUR GOD...
AND I LOVE YOU MORE THAN YOU KNOW!
NEVER FORGET I AM YOUR FATHER,
SO I'D LIKE TO SEE YOUR INNER LIGHT GLOW.

I AM HERE FOR YOU ALL THE TIME,
SO, HAVE NO FEAR MY CHILD,
BECAUSE YOU WILL ALWAYS BE MINE.

9/12/02
-Will Holmes Jr.

Not Like A Prayer [Introduction]

Poetry has become widely known as a method of healing for people. Unfortunately, even poetry is not like a prayer.

I know that sometimes you may feel like there's not a prayer in you. We all feel like that at times, but what we're really saying is that we feel like we can't talk to God. It just so happens that those are the times when we need to talk to Him the most because it's likely that there's something that's not right in our life. If you feel intimidated by The Father, then talk to His Son, Jesus. And if nobody else understands (including you), He understands. After all, he's been here before. Talk to Him. Cry to Him. Beg Him. Holler (but don't curse Him). Ask Him. Tell Him... whatever...

Any communication is better than no communication.
Maybe you don't know how to talk to God. Don't feel bad. One of Jesus' disciples had to ask Jesus to teach them to pray (Luke 11:1).

Personally, when I pray, I'm usually very informal.

Not Like A Prayer

You can climb a million stairs
But it won't get you There
You won't even get closer
Because it's not like a prayer

You can call who you will
But don't expect them to care
You can call on the mayor
But it's not like a prayer

You can make a wish
But it's up to you to make it true
It's not on God's list
Of *"Things To Do:"*

You can blow out all the candles
You can look in the air
And wish on every shooting star
But it's not like a prayer

You can spend your life in school
Do all to prepare
And you still may not make it
Because it's not like a prayer

You can seek the world's wisest
Learn all you can bear
But in the end, all you'll know
Is that it's not like a prayer

...poem continued>

Lord Jesus please
Allow us Your presence
Show me the way
And teach me life's essence

Teach us what does
And what doesn't matter
Strengthen my spirit
So that I won't shatter

Let us remember
That You are the Teacher
That God is God
And that I am the creature

We cannot depend
On man's understanding
I'll call for You
When life is demanding

We've heard You have an ear
For each one of us
So Lord, will You help me
To do what I must?

We'll be Your believers
Brush off the dust
When I pray to You
Faith in You is showing my trust

We wasted our time
With a psychic soothsayer
Because all they could say
Was not like a prayer

Our work is in vain
Until prayer begins

In Your name Jesus
We pray
Amen.

8/5/01
-Éric L Farrell

Four Closure

I have come to realize my **significance**. And even though I am nowhere **near perfect**, I am able to receive God's **blessed assurance** through **my prayer**.

Significance [Introduction]

God, why am I here? I don't like it here.

Sometimes we lose hope of ever finding solace. Usually, we give up right before God reaches us, which can be tragic. Sometimes we just need to find our purpose in the world. It's always there, but it's not always apparent.

Some of us love God, but if we don't realize our reason for being here on earth, this life can seem meaningless. Some of us Christians have even begun to think that our sole purpose for being on earth is to praise God. However, if our only purpose was to praise God, that wouldn't justify why we're here on earth. We can praise God in Heaven. Why would we need to be on earth? God has work for us to do on earth, and it is something we'll be able to enjoy doing (Ecclesiastes 2:24). In some way, He'll use us to make others' lives better here, while at the same time, providing us with pleasure in our work.

If you feel no reason to be on earth, then maybe you're not doing the work that God has set aside for you. Perhaps you need to *seek God to find out how to get more joy from the work you're currently doing* (Ecclesiastes 2:24). In Jesus' name, I promise your joyful work is out there. Search for it. And once you find it, you'll find yourself asking God to allow you to finish it before He takes you to Heaven. I can't promise you that you'll find it right away, but in due time you'll find it if you seek to please Him. We're now in a time when God seriously needs to use our lives. He wouldn't have made you if He didn't need you. It's time for you to begin to find out why He made you, then do what He's called you to do. Even if you can't see it now, just know that your life on earth does have significance.

Significance
(A Poetic Biography of Henry Russ)

I have a little story
That I would like to tell
Of love, life, blessings
And death as well

The pain was unbearable
It's hard to understand
As we look back
At the mind of a young man

He had lost something dear
And from this, lost hope
But thank God for the knot
At the end of the rope

A young lady had once
Held the key to his heart
Came break-up time
And they had to depart

She went her way
And he went his
But he was headed toward
The San Fran Bay Bridge

On his way
He stopped to say bye
To one last friend
Before he took to the sky

...poem continued>

This friend then looked him
Dead in his face
And asked if he would
Accept God's grace

But in place of those words
What he asked him then
Was, "Would you watch my shop?
A favor for a friend?"

Now the young man
Was not a pro with these cars
But he tinkered and he toyed
And he fixed a few parts

Hours went by
As he forgot about time
He forgot his old love
And the stress on his mind

Previously
He just wanted escape
From the broken-heartedness
So his life, he would take

His friend came back
When night was near
And he asked the young man
"Are you still here?"

The young man said,
"I fell in love with this art
I tinkered and I toyed
And I fixed this part!"

Still on his way
Caught the bus to his death
It was now nighttime
As he took a deep breath

He thought about how
His pain disappeared
As he tinkered and he toyed
Till his heart was re-geared

He thought about all
The things he would miss
He thought about that
And he thought about this

The girl might have had
The key to his heart
But he had found another way
To "make the car start"

But he was still on his way
To San Francisco's Bay
But this is not where God
Would have him stay

The bus light was on
But no one could see
The pain in his eyes
Where he would soon be

To look out the window
He looked to the right
And what he saw next
Would change his life

...poem continued>

He saw an old man
In the reflection of his eyes
And it stirred his soul
The old man was alive!

The old man said,
"I fell in love with this art
When God tinkered and toyed
And fixed my heart!"

And all of a sudden
A sudden change of plan
He crossed the bridge
From a boy to a man!

Now just think for a minute
If the light wasn't on
Would the reflection and the old man
That told this be gone?

dedicated to Henry Russ (1918 - 2002)
  a true story

4/27/99
-Éric L Farrell

Near Perfect [Introduction]

Some of us make the mistake of never accepting anything less than perfection.

This can cause us to miss out on enjoying the many great people and things in our lives, just because we want perfection. I'm not saying we should settle for less, but we should learn to appreciate what we ARE blessed with in life before it's gone.

Near Perfect

To chase down Perfection,
Many are in the hunt.
But it's not a need,
It's a want.
Nobody's perfect,
Though many deceive.
It's an unreachable goal,
Impossible to achieve.*
Try to reach for too much,
You might lose what you have now,
Appreciate what you got,
Before you forget how.

5/26/98
-Will Holmes Jr.

*Perfection in God's sight is possible through Christ. (John 17:23)

Blessed Assurance [Introduction]

Have you ever felt like you were in a disastrous situation, doomed in your own personal hurricane with no shelter?

Are you a child of God? Remember that God will never leave you nor forsake you. And when the Lord is with you in the midst of the storm, you can walk on water. All you must do is stay focused on Him, no matter what. God will help you through any of life's storms. Believe That!

24 But the ship was now in the midst of the sea, tossed with waves: for the wind was contrary... 29 And he (Jesus) said, COME. And when Peter was come down out of the ship, he walked on the water, to go to Jesus.

-Matthew 14:24,29

Blessed Assurance

When times get rough, just look at Me
And if you have to, even stare
But nevertheless, by faith, not sight
Just know I always care

I know you've heard them say
I won't give more than you can bear
And if I could bear it, then so can you
Look to your left son, I'm right here.

12/16/01
-Éric L Farrell

"Behold, what manner of love the Father hath bestowed upon us, that we should be called the sons of God..."

-1 John 3:1

My Prayer [Introduction]

I've heard many times from people that they just don't know how to pray.

They are willing, but just can't find the words to say to God. And, it's true. Sometimes it's not always as easy as it may seem. But in Matthew 6:5-16, Jesus teaches us how to pray. It's not hard at all. It doesn't have to be formal (as my partner E has stated in *"Not Like A Prayer"*). Just talk to God like you would your best friend. The following is my personal but general "prayer poem," which was my way of making prayer easier. Maybe it can help guide you in your prayer life as well.

My Prayer

Dear Lord,
Give me the wisdom to understand and help my sister and
  my brother.
Continue to fill me with love towards my father and my
  mother.
Lord, give me the strength to accept life's challenges,
And give me the understanding
To make it through the trials and the balances.
Give me the knowledge of right and wrong,
And give me the power to hold on and be strong.

Carry me through the valleys; lead me beside the waters,
And climb beside me to the mountain peak.
Lord, give me the ear to listen,
So I can hear You when You speak,
And give me the endurance when the road becomes steep.
Please give me the answers when it's You I seek.

Order my steps in what You would have me to do.
Give me the eyes,
So I may see what's false and what's true.
Allow Your light to shine through me, so that all may see.
Give me the faith to fight off the Devil's attacks,
So I can be what You want me to be.

Lord, give me the courage to change the things I can,
And bless me with the comfort of knowing who I am.
Lead me on the road of success in my life.
Surround me with great friendships,
And match me with a loving and beautiful wife.

Lord, give me the humility to stay modest when I do great
  things.
Help me to pass up what temptation brings.
Lord, give me the motivation to seek You deeper,
And fill me with praise for You,
Knowing You are my keeper.
And, Lord, please give of Yourself as my friend,
In the name of Your Son Jesus, I pray...Amen.

12/15/98
-Will Holmes Jr.

Salvation

(To receive Jesus as your Saviour, say these words aloud and believe)

I am a sinner.
Christ Jesus, you are the Lord.
I know the cost of sin is death
So thank you for paying mine with your blood.
I give you my soul for this favor.
You died on the cross on my behalf
So I receive you and confess you as Lord and Saviour.
You saved me from condemnation and wrath.
I believe in my heart that God raised You, His Son, from
*   the dead.*
Thank you.
Through faith in your name, I now have eternal life
Because my death was paid by you...
When you offered up yourself as the Sacrifice
Once and for all. Amen.

Speak the words above with your mouth, and believe them in your heart, and receive peace and comfort through faith in God, knowing He will never depart. If you've ever sold your soul to the Devil, then Christ can buy it back. As a counter-attack, He died for that. If you've led others the wrong way, then lead them back with the help of your siblings in Christ, we'll get them on the right track. Fear man no more, because we roll with the Lord and we already know the end! When all is said and done, and the Devil has had his so-called "fun," he'll eat defeat, while we go home with the Win!   -Éric L Farrell

John 3:16; Romans 3:10,23; Romans 5:8; Romans 6:23; Romans 10:13; John 1:12; I Corinthians 15:3-4; Revelation 3:20; 1 Thessalonians 5:8-11

Romans 10:9; John 5:24; John 20:31; I John 5:13; Hebrews 10:4

Behind the Poems ...

The Tale of Many Men [Behind the Poem]

This poem was written after going too far with a female with whom I was involved. I'm a witness that you don't have to have sex in order for your spirit to mix with someone else's. No, you don't have to go "all the way." It wasn't a coincidence that Will was trying to call me at the exact same time I was messing up, playing with temptation. God has a way of getting us out of sticky situations (1 Corinthians 10:13). No, Will didn't ever get through to me. But immediately after I knew I went too far, I got a call from home because my job required me to immediately leave town for the summer. I had to start my internship a week earlier than originally planned. Yes, I felt slapped by God. And although I got in trouble with God, I knew He sent me away to keep me out of trouble. Now I only had time to pack and tie up loose ends at home. That was the last day I saw her that summer.

We ended up establishing a platonic friendship, but I quickly discovered that a part of her was still with me. It was the part of her that had a problem with lustful thoughts. The problem of lust was not completely new to me, but now it had returned after teaming up with her's to become something more devastating. I had to crawl back to God with prayer and fasting to get my spirit clean again. I've crawled back to God more than once. This was my battle, but when I laid it in front of God, it became His battle, and God's battles are already won.

For some of you, it's drugs; for some of you, it's alcohol; and for some, it's food or something else. You know the thing that kills you inside that you just can't seem to beat with your own strength. It takes more than just going on a "seven-day, break free plan." It takes supernatural strength. It takes the type of strength that you can only get from God. When you accepted Christ as your Saviour (p. 80), this is what you got saved from (also saved from death). When you realize the purpose that God has for your life, you'll realize how much those vices hinder you from doing your job for God. Then you'll see the true importance of staying free from them. When you go back to what you are freed from, you transgress and break your bond with God. You'll have to go back to God and repent and ask for His strength to be with you again. Don't just ask for forgiveness, but ask Him to give you the strength and a purpose to change your life. When He does, remember how good it feels to be free. In case you should ever transgress again, you can remember that your freedom feels much better than your bondage. Never hesitate to repent, and repent because you want to be free. Remember that doing what you want to do and doing what makes you happy are not always the same thing. Do what will make you happy. Stay free.

"For if I build again the things which I destroyed, I make myself a transgressor" (Galatians 2:18).

"*The Tale of Many Men*" was born on July 9, 2000 at my apartment in Richmond, VA. It was originally composed electronically with the purpose of being sent through E&W Collaborations. My personal struggle poems are the ones that receive the most gratitude from others. I'm sure this is because all of us have experienced a personal struggle. However, when we share our testimonies with others, we begin to realize that our struggle is not as personal as we thought. You are not alone, because "*this same has been the story and the tale of*" all of us.

In July 2000, this poem was partially recorded online and may still be heard at www.ericlfarrell.com. It was first performed on Armistice Day, November 11, 2000 at the Baptist Student Union's Coffee House of Virginia Union University.

Psalm 25   Galatians 2:18
Luke 15:18-24   Matthew 12:43-45
I Corinthians 6:13-20; 10:11-13   James 1:12-16
Romans 3:23   Proverbs 13:15

This poem (page 22) was SENT through E&W for July 2000.

Sometimes We Fall [Behind the Poem]

At some points in my life, I have felt like I was spiritually asleep. I felt like I had lost my tight bond with the Lord. Not necessarily because I was falling into sin, but I was drifting. I wasn't maintaining my relationship or communication with God. I was just going day to day... "spiritually sleepwalking." This poem came at a time after I had reached a spiritual high point in my life. I felt like I had the faith to move mountains, and the connection with God to receive anything I asked for in prayer. But something happened. Slowly and gradually, I lost that relationship with God. It seemed like one day I was on a spiritual high, and before I realized it, the next day I had lost that connection with Him. I felt like I had lost my purpose in life. I just got up everyday and went through the daily routine. Life was not necessarily going bad, but I just felt out of touch spiritually and mentally. I realized it. I recognized it. I heard sermons about it. But I just kept sleep walking. One day, I received an e-mail from a friend who sent out e-mails of spiritual encouragement. Her message that day was about breaking out of spiritual darkness NOW and getting yourself back on track. I made the decision that day to get back in line and start praying and studying my Word again to regain my spiritual strength. The alarm had finally awaken me.

That experience helped me to think back to my own experiences and the experiences of others. I realized that many people go through periods in their lives when they lose touch with God. Unfortunately, for some, this means falling into sinful and unhealthy actions and relationships.

Usually, when we fall, there are those close to us that try to help us break out of these actions or relationships. But, since we are "sleep-walking," we disregard their advice and continue to backslide and fall. The Bible tells us that everyone has sinned and fallen short of God's glory. So, if you have fallen, it is not too late for you to get back up and get right with God again. We have to be cautious, because the decisions that we make are usually what lead us into our downfalls. For example, you may end up in an unhealthy relationship in which you easily fall for the temptation of sexual sin and you're negatively influenced by your partner overall. But it all started from your decision to date that person. You dated them even though you knew they didn't understand your values, views, and lifestyle.

When we fall, it's either because of our decisions, or because we've compromised our morals, standards, or beliefs. When we do that, we leave ourselves vulnerable for the enemy's attack on our body and spirit.

Also, when we fall, it's not always easy to get back up again. And if we have to make extra efforts, sometimes we just become content where we are. Then, we fall so deep that we don't even realize how bad things are for us. That's why we have to force ourselves to get back up again.

Ask God for help, strength, direction, and guidance. Even if you "don't feel like it," read your Bible and pray. Do everything you can to reestablish your relationship with God. And most importantly, you must pay attention to the advice of those close to you. They are the ones that care - the ones that usually know you the best and can tell when you're falling into things that are not good for you.

Don't allow sinful ways, actions, people, and relationships to keep you under control. Do your best to stay in God's will, continually seeking to be more Christ-like. But if you fall, do everything you can to "get back up again."

Psalm 25; James 1:22-25, 4:6-10; Luke 22:40

This poem (page 26) was SENT through E&W for May 2001.

Going Through [Behind the Poem]

This poem was born on Saturday, May 20, 2000. At this time in my life, I had just finished my Junior year at Virginia Union University and was about to begin a successful internship at DuPont. This poem was originally written with the purpose of being sent through E&W Collaborations.

Is the thought behind this poem (p. 29) similar to Yin Yang? ☯

No. Yin Yang is a Chinese principle that basically states that two equal, opposing energies (black and white) work together to bring balance to everything in the world. However, we know that all things do not *work together to balance out.* We know that no amount of evil can ever balance out God's good. We know that all things are not simply black and white or good and bad. "And we know that all things *work together for good to them that love God,* to them who are the called according to his purpose" (Romans 8:28). So instead of things happening to cause a balanced world, things happen to cause a world that is favorable to us who love God, so that we're useful in helping to accomplish His purpose.

Ephesians 1:9-11; Romans 8:28; 2 Corinthians 4:15-17; Luke 6:20-25

This poem (page 29) was SENT through E&W for May 2000.

Experience [Behind the Poem]

I've always loved quotes. In fact, I've even begun to write my own book of quotes. This poem came about while trying to write a simple quote about life experiences. Even when writing only a few words, it's always hard to hold back the urge to make my words rhyme. In this case, the rhyme side of my mind got the best of me, and turned this quote into a poem. In almost every situation, I've thought back to this poem before classifying my situation as "good" or "bad."

The original title was *"Experience, Chalked Up,"* which served as a reminder to take any seemingly bad experience in life and "chalk it up" as a learning experience. Indecisively, the title was again changed to *"Experience, Chalking It Up,"* before I finally said, "forget it," and simply named it *"Experience."*

An example of a situation that this poem would relate to is Luke 23:32-43. Here, a felon is promised eternal life while dying on the cross next to Jesus. I'm sure the felon thought this was his worse experience in life, but yet, it turned out to be his best, because this same day he went to Paradise with Jesus.

This poem was born on October 24, 1998, and presented at WordStage Poetry Lounge on November 9, 2002.

Luke 23:32-43; 2 Corinthians 4:8-18; Ecclesiastes 2:4-11; Luke 24:7,52

This poem (page 32) was SENT through E&W for October 2000.

No Escape [Behind the Poem]

The inspiration behind this poem is one of the more interesting among my selections in this book. I wrote this poem over a period of two years. When I first started it, I had made a choice in my life that I had prayed about and decided was the right choice. When I prayed, I asked God to work my situation out smoothly if my decision was in line with His will. Things were pretty much the exact opposite. I continued on in my decision though, because it was what I wanted to do. I just tried to make my decision "work" along with God's will. Even though I never felt completely comfortable with my decision, I tried to justify it with reasons why it was right. When I look back, I think that God was telling me to choose the opposite of what I chose, but I was blinded by my own desires at the time. Well, I started to write this poem as my situation started to become worse because of my decision. But I still had hope that things would turn around, so I was kind of torn between whether or not I had made the right choice.

When I write my poetry, my best works are usually the ones that I just sit down and write out completely (and then maybe edit a little bit later). When I struggle with the words for any length of time, then I usually give up on the poem. I feel like my best works are those that are truly inspired so that I feel like God is speaking through me with my words on paper. So, when the words don't come quickly, I assume that I'm forcing the poem with my own will, and not letting true inspiration work through me. Well, when I started this poem, it didn't flow. I found it later and continued some more, and once again lost the flow.

This poem just didn't leave me alone. As I continued to go through the situation, I kept coming back to this poem and adding more to it. Finally, I wrote the last words: "But you've got to move on... / 'cause once the storm is over, The sun will shine bright."

Almost three years later, I came to a conclusion. I realized that my decision in that situation was not in line with God's will. I saw the different ways that He was trying to speak to me to tell me to deal with that situation differently than I desired. And that's when I finished writing this poem (which I came back to once again – I guess you could say I couldn't *escape* this poem!). There were several lessons learned in that experience. In some ways, I still feel like I never did escape. I continue to look back at how I could have handled the situation differently; how much better it could have turned out if I had truly followed God's will instead of my own desires. But, I also realize that that experience helped me to grow and see things that I would have otherwise missed. God used my mistake for my own benefit. Even as I write these words now, I am comforting myself, so I hope these words and this poem bring comfort to you.

Allow God to lead you in your life's choices, and the road to happiness and success will be a lot less bumpy. Pray that you don't take God's will and try to somehow align it with your own desires. And make sure you don't hide from God's will by pretending not to know what choice He wants you to make.

God definitely hears our prayer requests and knows our desires, but sometimes He warns us or tries to lead us in another direction. We must gain the humility to become followers of His way and not leaders of ourselves.

Isaiah 55:6-9; Luke 6:46-49; Psalms 145:18,19

This poem (page 34) was SENT through E&W for January 2002.

I'm Maintaining [Behind the Poem]

I guess you could say this poem was inspired by my favorite T-shirt. The front of the shirt shows a man's head and hands popping out between the waves of a lake. One hand is desperately reaching out and the other hand is holding a pencil. The back of the shirt features the rest of the man's body dangling under water struggling to stay afloat. Underwater with him and all around him, are various symbols and pictures that represent many of the wrongful and evil things going on in this world today. I guess you could say it's like a pool of destruction, the world, or just life itself. The word "MAINTAINING" is above the picture. That's what the man is doing. With all that's going on around him, even with his "life" trying to drown him, he is "maintaining." I could seriously relate to this shirt, especially since the man was holding a pencil. I assume he's a writer, and he's using his writing to help him maintain, like I do. Life is the inspiration for my poetry and my poetry is what I use to maintain, and to deliver a message to help others maintain.

This poem was written during a point in my life in which some things weren't going as I would have liked. But I realized that no matter what I was going through or what could go wrong, I was still maintaining. I still had my faith. I still had my Lord. I still had Jesus. And just knowing that, should help anyone to realize an important fact: No matter what you are going through, everything is perfect in your life as long as you are maintaining your faith and your relationship with Jesus. So that became my trademark response. "Hey, how you doing Will?" – "I'm maintaining." Such a simple answer, but to me, it said so much.

No matter what feelings or emotions your life may be bringing out of you; no matter what experiences and burdens life is putting on you; no matter who turns their back on you when you need them most... you can always turn to Jesus. And with Him, you'll be able to maintain and keep your head above water without drowning.

The poem is representative of some of the experiences and emotions that a person can go through. They range from the every-day experiences, to some of the most deepest and darkest feelings. The man in this poem goes through just about everything, but he continues to maintain. He doesn't know why he must endure this pain. He doesn't know how it's possible that he hasn't lost his mind or his life yet. Sometimes we don't realize it, but God is always there for us and never leaves us. As the person in this poem realizes, if we maintain our faith, then we can also maintain our peace, sanity, and happiness.

Deuteronomy 31:6; Psalms 40:1-4; Romans 8:28

This poem (page 37) was SENT through E&W for December 1999.

Losing A Loved One [Behind the Poem]

The holidays are supposed to be a time of rejoicing and happiness, but one year they became a time of shock and mourning for my family. That's what inspired this poem.

During the holiday season of Thanksgiving and Christmas of 1998, my Aunt and Uncle (my dad's sister and brother) passed away within a period of six weeks. My Aunt Ruby died right before Thanksgiving, and about a month later, my Uncle Allen died before Christmas. I wrote this poem after my Aunt's death. It was very hard for me to endure at the time, because I remember wanting to leave college to go home for Thanksgiving. My family wanted to travel to South Carolina to visit relatives. But Her death meant that I would now be going home, which I wanted badly, but definitely not like that. I started feeling guilty for even wanting to go home.

They were in a car accident together. Right after the accident, my Uncle later told the family that my Aunt Ruby got out of the car to walk around and check on him. He survived the accident, but soon after they reached the hospital, she died from internal bleeding and injuries. A few weeks later, my Uncle's condition became worse. It was discovered that he had lung cancer. My Uncle and Aunt were very close, so I'm sure the sadness from suddenly losing his sister in the car accident didn't help his health at all. After his death, right before Christmas, my Uncle Marvin (my dad's last sibling) died two years later, after he became ill as well. He suffered a heart attack while in the hospital.

Death and funerals don't necessarily have to be a time of sadness and grief. They should be a time to look back at all the reasons why you will miss that person so much, not times to be sad that you can't share them anymore. Be happy that you were able to share those moments. Not to mention, they are now enjoying the good life in Heaven with our Lord!

This poem is dedicated in loving memory of my Aunt Ruby Jones, Uncle Allen Holmes, Uncle Marvin Holmes, and to all those that have experienced losing family and friends suddenly, and without warning.

This poem is especially dedicated to my Dad, who lost all of his siblings in a period of three years.

Romans 14:7-9

This poem (page 41) was SENT through E&W for November 1999 with *"Fair Life?"*

Fair Life? [Behind the Poem]

The inspiration for this poem came at a point in my life when there were certain things I wanted out of life. (note: they were not "needs" at the time, but "wants.")

I looked around at friends and associates who were receiving and achieving the things that I wanted. It seemed so unfair to me. I couldn't figure out why I was the only one who wasn't getting what I wanted. Was I doing something wrong? I figured I was living by God's will as much as, if not more, than they were. So why was I the only one getting overlooked for what I wanted and prayed for? I began realizing that nobody ever said life was fair.

God never promised that to us. He never told us that we will all get the same thing, the same way, at the same time. What God did say is that He will bless us with the desires of our heart according to His will. He teaches us not to envy the possessions of others, but to be thankful for what we have. Also, He said that all things will work out for our good. And that is what happened to me.

When I look back, some of the things I wanted would not have been good for me to have at THAT point in time. God did not open my eyes to this until much later though. I looked at the things I DID HAVE, that others did NOT, and I realized how blessed I actually was. I believe that God distributes gifts and blessings to different people at different times, because it's what they may need at that time. Sometimes, we look at someone else and want what they have. At the same time, they're looking at us and desiring something in our life that we don't even recognize or appreciate. That's why I say be thankful for what you DO have, not upset about what you DON'T have.

I can honestly say, that I eventually received the things I wanted. But I received them in better packages, at better times in my life, when I was ready to receive them. So, we just have to wait on the Lord and keep faith that He will fulfill our desires if we continue to follow His will. There is a time and a season for everything.

Mark 11:24; Romans 8:28; John 16:20-23; Ecclesiastes 3:1

This poem (on p.43) was SENT through E&W for November 1999 with *"Losing A Loved One."*

Fear Less [Behind the Poem]

By now, you may know that I generally rebel against ways of living that are contrary to what God teaches us in the Bible. With this poem, I've sought to do just that. This poem is a product of a man who has turned his fear into anger toward ungodly things.

When I think of all the hardship that the Devil has unleashed on the people that I care about, it makes me want to take his head off. However, knowing that I can't defeat the Devil with my hands, I seek to beat him with the weapons and gifts that God has given to me. I'm sure it hurts the Devil when I turn down his temptations, when I pray, or when I simply love my neighbor as myself.

Just recently, I've begun to realize where fear comes from. I've recently heard of a study that was done on babies of about two years of age. In this study, the babies were made to watch a lady on videotape acting as if she was afraid of a ball. After watching the tape, the babies were presented with a ball to play with. However, the babies made sure to stay far away from it. Babies who had not seen the tape, fearlessly played with the ball. The other babies were taught to fear, just as we are taught to fear. I know you don't want me to say it, but the news programs are one way we're taught to fear. It's not a surprise, but it's not often admitted either. Scary movies are another way that we're taught to fear. They gradually teach us to fear the dark, spiders, the telephone and other things that we have no logical reason to be afraid of. We're no different than the baby with the ball. I know what you're thinking... "a telephone?" Yes, I'm sure you or someone you know has thought twice about answering the phone after watching the movie Scream.

There are dozens of movies I could name to prove my point, but fear of a telephone is the most illogical fear that I can think of at the time. I'm sure you may keep watching them. I won't say that I'll never watch a scary movie again, but the fact will always remain that we're teaching ourselves to fear at the same time we're asking God to keep us from being fearful.

But again I ask, "Why should I fear anything if I've got the Almighty God on my side?" My chant is this: "Yea, though I walk through the valley of the shadow of death, I shall fear no evil! Evil shall fear me!.. In the name of the Lord!"

Psalms 23:4; 27:1-3; 34:4; 56:2-4
Proverbs 29:25
Luke 12:4-5
1 Peter 3:12-14
Philippians 1:20-24, 27-28; 4:13
1 Samuel 17:32-51

I recorded "Fear Less" on the "Fearless" (EP) album by Gospel Hip Hop Artist, Rory Lyon of Wordlyf. I note Rory as my favorite rap artist for his rythmic lyrics and beats, matched with meaningful content, a throaty voice, and a humble spirit. "Fearless" was released in July 2003, as promotion for the release of "Aggressive," the group project by Wordlyf. Currently, it can be found at www.mp3.com/wordlyf

This poem (page 45) was SENT through E&W for November 2002.

It Shall Come To Pass [Behind the Poem]

To everything there is a season, as I've mentioned earlier in this book. There are seasons of blessings. Unfortunately, there are also seasons of downfall, unhappiness, sorrow, loneliness, financial instability, confusion, etc. It is during these seasons, that we look forward to our future blessings. We look forward to making it through the "storm" to experience "joy in the morning."

I have experienced several seasons in my life. I've experienced the highs and the lows. I wrote this poem in the midst of one of the low seasons. I knew that my faith would bring me through, but it was hard waiting for God to move. I started thinking: "Ok, Lord, I'm trusting you, but, um, this is taking kind of long here. Will my time ever come? If so, when?"

When we are awaiting answers to our questions, responses to our prayers, changes in our situations, and resolutions to our problems, we start to question God if we don't *see* a timely change occur. What we must realize is that we cannot expect God to deliver when we want. He is not on our time, we are on His time. And He may not come when we want Him to, but He'll always be right on time. I can definitely testify to that. God knows us better than we know ourselves. We may ask for this or that, but God knows what's best for us and when to bless us with it.

God spoke to me through this poem. The purpose is to provide to you the same comfort that God provided to me. I can also testify that shortly after I wrote this poem, God started delivering!

The more we learn how to be patient and keep faith that God is working in our lives, the more God will do for us. He will also seem to move quicker. Instead of questioning as to when God will move in our lives, let's start praising Him throughoutabou our storms and low seasons. Let's ask Him for the guidance, strength, understanding, and wisdom we need to wait out the night until He brings us joy in the morning.

Deuteronomy 28:1-15; Ecclesiastes 3:1

This poem (page 48) was SENT through E&W for November 2001.

Mr. Suicide Bomber [Behind the Poem]

This poem was written to inform others of how people of different religions may see the world, while at the same time, providing an example of how we as Christians should treat them with love and understanding. Unfortunately, we often avoid asking others about their beliefs because we fear that we'll have to disagree or that they'll disagree with us. We must learn that we don't have to agree with someone in order to come to a better understanding of them. Remember that communication is a two-way conversation and that love conquers all.

How Should We Deal with People of Other Religions?
I'll worry about a man before I hate him. Everything we do, should be done in love. We must be watchful of how we talk to others, because "a soft answer turneth away wrath: but grievous words stir up anger" (Proverbs 15:1). If we see our conversations with people as arguments to be won, then we'll always lose. If we win an argument to prove our belief to be correct, but leave the other person feeling like a loser, then we've just lost that person. If we lose the person, then we've actually lost. No matter what religion they profess, we must love them as a person first and foremost. We shouldn't try to lead people to salvation for the purpose of making ourselves look good or to earn heavenly points. Instead, we should do it because we love the person and want them to inherit the Kingdom of God with us. Our purpose is not necessarily for Christ to win their souls, but for their souls to win Christ. Without sincerity of heart, we're seen as Christian recruiters. And without sincerity, that's all we are.

Yes, my Christian belief will conflict with their belief. But whether or not they accept what I say, they should know that I'm only telling them because I love them.

This poem was written on September 12th, of 2002; one day and one year after the September 11th Attacks.

Hebrews 12:14; Romans 13:8-12; Proverbs 15:1-2; Ecclesiastes 9:18

This poem (page 52) was SENT through E&W for September 2002.

Genocide [Behind the Poem]

This poem was inspired by the actions and words of the people here in America, concerning the attacks of September 11th.

On October 8th of 2001, this was written to be a voice of reason in a time of chaos –the chaos that existed within the minds of the American people and others. This poem speaks about our hasty assumptions and unstable minds. We revert to these assumptions when trying to handle the situation ourselves. All too often, we assume that God is not going to do His job, so we panic. Instead, we must have faith in Him.

And we must remember our *soul purpose* for being on earth, which is to love others. We want their souls to be saved and their minds to be comforted. Will you boast about what God has given you, or will you use it to seek to better the lives of those who have not? Will you be prideful of your inherited comfortable living conditions, or will you show compassion to those who were born without? *"Either compassion or pride..."* choose one.

GOD BLESS THE WORLD.

Genocide was SENT through E&W on November 6, 2001. It was posted on the *Def Poetry Jam* website for January 2002, and first performed at G&A Productions' *Jazz Poetry Café* on April 10th in Stafford, VA. On May 3rd of 2002, it was recited at the *Nuyorican Poets Café* in New York in dedication to all lost on September 11th.

"Dearly beloved, avenge not yourselves, but rather give place unto wrath: for it is written, VENGEANCE IS MINE; I WILL REPAY, saith the Lord. Therefore if thine enemy hunger, feed him; if he thirst, give him drink: for in so doing thou shalt heap coals of fire on his head. Be not overcome of evil, but overcome evil with good." -Romans 12:19-21

Proverbs 16:5-8; John 16:3; Romans 12:9-21; 13:8-13; Nahum 1:2-7

This poem (page 56) was SENT through E&W for October 2001.

Lord, Why? [Behind the Poem]

This poem was written the day after *September 11th* of 2001, a day which will go down in history as "Nine–Eleven" (9-11).

On this day, America suffered one of its greatest tragedies in history. The World Trade Center Towers in New York City and the Pentagon in Washington, D.C. were attacked by suicide terrorists in jet airplanes. The WTC Towers crumbled to the ground. The Pentagon was heavily damaged. Over 3,000 people lost their lives. Families lost their fathers, mothers, sons, and daughters. Our fear and anxiety rose to high levels. Many people wouldn't even step foot onto an airplane, and some still won't.

All of this damage and loss of loved ones made it hard for people to believe that God was still in control and watching over them and their families. Many people questioned, "Lord, why did this happen?" Several other *"Lord, why?"* questions also arose across the nation. This poem is a representation of a question-answer session with God. It not only symbolizes our questions since 9-11, but also the questions we had before 9-11.

Life can be hard to accept. So as humans, the hardships and confusion of life leave us to question God. At worst, it causes some to lose trust and faith in God. But everything unpleasant that happens is not the lack of God's power but the presence of evil. In the story of Job, the Devil tries to show God that Job is only a faithful servant because Job's life is going well. The Devil says that if God allows him (the Devil) the opportunity to make Job sick, take his family, and damage his livelihood, then Job will no longer be happy and faithful. God allows this as long as the Devil doesn't take Job's life. His faith and strength overpower the Devil's attacks in the end, and God rewards Job double what he had before.

When life hits us with hard blows, how do we react? Do we continue to trust God? Or do we give up on God and lose our faith?

We need to realize that God is and always will be on the throne, and that His ways and thoughts are higher than ours. Even if God answered ALL of our questions, we still wouldn't be able to grasp and understand how He accomplishes His purpose. We just have to keep our faith throughout the trials, tribulations, storms, and hardships of life. As we keep our faith, we must also maintain our joy and praise for the Lord. Life is not designed to be problem-free, but God will work it out perfectly. No matter how "in line" you are with God's will and how smoothly you think your life should run, you will always face some type of hardship. Everyone must live with and push forward with the "hand they are dealt." Use your hardship as your testimony, and throughout all, God will always stand by you. He will always be there to comfort you and bring you through. We need to maintain our relationship with Him, so when hard times hit, we are prepared and able to recover, and even help others.

1 Peter 3:12-15; Isaiah 55:6-9; Job 2:1-6; 42:10-12

The poem (page 59) was SENT through E&W for September 2001.

Not Like A Prayer [Behind the Poem]

This poem was written on August 5th of 2001, for myself as well as others. I believe God gave me this poem as His reminder for me to spend more time in prayer.

In today's busy society, it's so easy to neglect ourselves of prayer time. Part of the reason for this is that many of us have evolved into multi-taskers. Some of us have even learned to read our Bible while paying attention to the preacher. However, prayer is something that can't be effectively multi-tasked. Sure, the quick fix prayer while we're in the car may be fine for the moment, but that's not the time that God is likely to reach us. We need to take time away from all of life's little distractions and focus on speaking *with* Him. From what I read, Jesus did a lot of serious praying. He prayed all night at times; and He was Jesus! How much more do we need to pray?

Please read the scriptures below to learn a little more about prayer.

Matthew 6:5-8	(Pray in sincerity, not with repetition or for show)
Luke 6:12-13; Acts 6:3-5	(Pray before decisions, especially big ones)
Luke 18:1-8; Acts 12:5	(Pray continually)
Philippians 4:6	(Thank God along with your prayerful requests)
2 Chronicles 7:12-15	(God is waiting for us to pray, so that He can help us)
Luke 18:9-14	(A valuable story - Prayer is not the time to act righteous)
Luke 11:1	("Lord, teach us to pray...")
Matthew 6:9-13	(The Lord's Prayer)
James 5:13-18	(Prayer influences things)

This poem (page 62) was SENT through E&W for April 2002.

Significance [Behind the Poem]

First, I'll say that the sentiment of this story cannot be communicated with words. This poem was written on April 27th of 1999, after meeting a man by the name of Henry Russ (1918-2002) and hearing his life story. How did this happen? I'll tell you...

My car was giving me grief, so I had to take it somewhere to get it fixed. There was one problem. I had no idea what was wrong with the car and I didn't have a mechanic I could trust. I didn't want to be "taken for a ride," so I asked around and finally got a referral from Will's brother-in-law. "Tell 'em Jonathan Coleman sent you," he said, as he directed me to Russ' Sales and Service on the corner of Leigh and Boulevard. That's where I met Henry Russ. Yes, this 82 year old man was about to climb under my car and fix it. Andrew Rogers, a brother of ours, drove there with me to give me a ride back to campus. As we went through the paperwork with Henry in his back office, we somehow got on the topic of God and how He takes care of us. Soon, Andrew and I found ourselves wide-eyed and attentive as we listened to the life story of Henry Russ.

We were sitting in the presence of an elderly man, who once had plans to die young. During a visit to California, he was going to kill himself by jumping off San Francisco's Golden Gate Bridge, the #1 location in the world for suicides. I remember him telling me that his attempt happened before the suicide-prevention mesh was installed on that bridge in 1937. After writing this poem, I took it back to the shop and gave it to Henry Russ. After reading it, he looked at me... "This is amazing, this is exactly right, it's so accurate!" he said.

I didn't listen to his story with the purpose of writing a poem, but it stuck with me. And prayerfully, it will stick with you.

Before my first book was published, I came home from college and ran into an old friend from junior high school. As I accompanied my grandmother in the hospital emergency room, I reacquainted with Desmond Johnson's ex-girlfriend. My grandmother recovered, but Desmond never gave himself the chance to recover from whatever he was facing. Desmond was a friend of mine from junior high school. "Desmond killed himself," are the words that she shocked me with. "I can't have this," I said to myself. "I can't allow people to feel that they'd have to do such a thing. I have to make some kind of change in peoples' lives." This propelled me into completing my first book, Verbalizions of Enlightenment: The Secret to the Pain.

Henry Russ decided to live. Maybe if Desmond had the chance to talk to Henry, or at least hear his story, he would have decided to live also.

"Significance" is in this book because Henry is no longer here to tell his story, but it still needs to be told. I believe that God will allow a Desmond to hear this story and decide to live to see old age, and one day tell his own story. Do you know a Desmond? Are you a Desmond? You need to live, because somebody needs to hear your story.

You may remember a hit song by Otis Redding, "Sitting on the Dock of the Bay." A couple of years after writing "Significance," I realized what his song was really about.

Life is What He Gave

A man with no more hope at the end of his rope, who saw no way out of his pain. He went to end his life, to try to end his strife, because he thought he had nothing to gain. But he did. He had a life to live, and he had someone else's to save. He could either live to tell his story and save necessary lives, or he could take it to his grave. He told his story, and if that's all he did, then the world is thankful today. A historical figure? No, he's much bigger, because *life* is what he gave.

-EL Farrell (2003)

Thank you Henry. Thank you Otis. Thank you Job. Thank all of you others who have chosen to live to tell your story.

Job 17:1; 19:6-21; 42:12-17

note: *Russ' Sales and Service* is still in operation and currently being run by Henry's grandson, Brad.

Near Perfect [Behind the Poem]

Too many of us are missing out on great husbands, wives, friendships, business deals, job opportunities and life experiences, because we look past what is average or good, trying to look for something perfect. I knew a friend of mine in a relationship that had a great foundation. However, like many couples, they had been through some challenges that started to tear them apart. So, even though he knew she was the best woman for him, he began to look elsewhere. I told him, "Don't pass up a GOOD thing, looking for the next BEST thing." If you don't understand that, then you won't get it on the way home, but hopefully you'll get it by the end of this book. What I actually should have told him was, "Don't miss your BLESSING looking for PERFECTION." In other words, don't miss out on what God has for you or what He wants to bless you with, because you keep looking for something perfect. Nothing is perfect. Nobody is perfect. Don't let anyone ever tell you different, but there are things and people that God blesses us with, according to what's best for us. If everyone falls short of God's glory, then none of us are even close to being perfect (Romans 3:23). Yet, we still expect to receive nothing but perfection. Something average to another, can be perfect for us individually.

I've seen this mindset have the most damage in jobs and relationships. People end up unemployed, unsatisfied, unhappy, lonely and in bad relationships. We must realize that what God blesses you with may not be perfect, but it may just be perfect for you. This poem encouraged me to look past the imperfections in a person or situation to see the perfect package that God had sent to me.

Most importantly, this mindset can also affect our relationship with God. People think if they aren't perfect, then they aren't ready to come to God and submit to Him. Wrong. When we're the furthest from being perfect, then that's when we need to come to Christ, so that He can make us perfect in God's sight. (John 17:23)

Romans 3:23; John 17:23

Blessed Assurance [Behind the Poem]

Originally written as inspiration to an incarcerated friend, this poem has more than one purpose. On two occasions, I found this poem to be the perfect wedding gift to close friends of mine to provide encouragement during tough times. It was coupled with a photograph I once took of the Atlantic Ocean, which I call "In the Midst of the Storm." In fact, this picture was taken from a hotel at Virginia Beach which recently (2003) met the destruction of Hurricane Isabel. In the picture that I took, it looks like there is a storm arising. When I think about this poem, I think about that picture because it reminds me of when Peter walked on water in the midst of the storm in order to go to Jesus (Matthew 14:23-31). As long as Peter had faith, Jesus brought him across the troubled waters, but when he saw the wind get worse, he got afraid and began to doubt. When he doubted then he began to sink.

This poem is meant to encourage you to keep your faith in God when troubles arise. It lets us know that God is always with us, although it may be hard to see Him at times.

*Inspired by and written in a letter to a Brother in Christ and close friend, Jay-Are Shariff, at the time of his incarceration.

"Be careful (full of care or concern) for nothing; but in everything by prayer and supplication with thanksgiving let your requests be made known unto God." -Phillipians 4:6

Phillippians 4:6-9; Matthew 14:23-31

My Prayer [Behind the Poem]

The Bible says that the prayers of the righteous are heard and avail much (1 Peter 3:12; James 5:16). So we know prayer is very valuable and beneficial, but how can we benefit from it if we don't pray?

Before I sat down to write this, I prayed. Nothing wordy. I asked, "Lord, please lead and guide me in writing this 'Behind the Poem' section for the 'My Prayer' poem. Please speak through my words so that it can help someone in their prayer life. In the name of your Son, Jesus, I pray. Amen." That's it. My thoughts put into prayer form.

You're not taking a verbal test when you pray to our Father. God already knows what you need before you ask (Matthew 6:8). I think He just wants to know if you'll ask Him for it. Now don't get me wrong; some prayers can be long. It's all about what's on your mind, and how you want to express it. But we shouldn't be intimidated into thinking that all our prayers have to be fancy to be heard. Like I said, the prayers of the righteous shall be heard. It doesn't say that long, structured prayers will be heard. (Matthew 6:7). Just never forget to pray "in the name of Jesus" our Saviour. In John 14:6, Jesus tells us we must go through him to get to His Father. Just the mentioning of the name Jesus holds power.

I was inspired to write this poem because I realized the importance of prayer, and that many people find it hard to pray or understand the power of prayer. Prayer is just an informal expression of your thoughts and feelings in a conversation with God. Prayer can be used to heal, protect, guide, empower, gain forgiveness, praise, open doors, and more. What would you like to use your prayers for today?

Join our mailing list

-get updates
-get our new monthly poems by e-mail

Visit:
www.ewcollaborations.com

If you don't have Internet or e-mail, send your name and address to:
Emaculate Publishing/ Attn: E&W/ PO Box 1074/ Woodbridge, VA 22195

Coming Soon... by Éric L Farrell

An Emaculate Author

Remember My Chains: From Africa to Now

"This book of poetry addresses, from a first person perspective, the struggles and heart-wrenching pain endured by the author and also by Blacks in general - transitioning from slavery until the present-day. The feelings and thoughts of a hopeless, yet determined people are projected by the author, so that you may empathize with, learn from, and be stengthened by such perseverance no matter what race or color you may be." **-Emaculate Publishing**

Excerpts from *Remember My Chains*

"...I couldn't prepare before I came to understand what I would hear They were screaming at me in a language completely foreign to my ear / I didn't have no family here, no friends to teach me about the process / No money to exchange, no means of family contact..."

from ... "In Concern of The Process:"

"...In doing this, we did our best, pushed on through all the mess, but nevertheless were never the less. We received no badge to bless our chest, but a badge is not why we progress..."

from... "In Faith"

"There was a time before I knew Africa / And before Africa knew me You see, Africa to me was not the other side of the sea / Africa to me was the other side of the tree / The tree that I heard tales of, that my forefathers hung from / My native land exists in the bosom of the equal people singing ~swing low sweet chariot~ song hums... So you see, Africa to me was not a place of far mileage / It was the place of peace on the other side of the tree of violence..."

from... "Africa to Me"

Verbalizions: Audiographed (poetry & music) - **coming soon...**

Coming Soon... by Charese Nicole

An Emaculate Author

An Abandoned Woman: Found by God

"This book of memoirs and poetry tells the authors resilient story of troubling hardships in relationships and marriage. This ordinary mother of two shares a magnificent testimony of how God saved and restored her in her darkest hour of despair. It will definitely reach the souls and hearts of young adults and women everywhere, whether single, separated, married, lonely, sad, miserable, hurt, or angry. As she continues on her journey of healing, she brings hope through the message that God has given her in the midst of her storms." **-Éric L Farrell, author & poet**

Excerpts from An Abandoned Woman

"...my husband of only three years decided he needed someone else to share his thoughts, dreams, and time with besides me... I admit, we didn't have the perfect relationship. We had arguments, disputes, and money issues, but what couple didn't? ....One Friday evening on my way home, I did the usual, picked the children up, stopped by the video store and went home. As I turned the key to open the door, I saw that my house was completely empty. He decided to leave and take EVERYTHING with him ....I began to feel the same way my home looked (empty)... not only did he take my heart, but he took sentimental things and left me with absolutley nothing. He actually stole everything I had left in me to keep going on!" *from... Chapter: The Broken Heart*

———————————————

"I've been burdened down for years, looking for a man to wipe away my tears, never had a father to calm my fears, so I trusted others with my heart to draw near. / A temporary relief was all it was, a moment of satisfaction just because... I needed someone to fill the void of this troubled heart..." *from... (untitled)*

"He is strengthening me in all areas of my life, revealing things to me that I never knew about Christ.... I'd rather be single, knowing and loving God, then to deal with emptiness, insecurity, broken promises and lies..." *from... "Singleness"*

Your Guidance Counselor recommends...

Verbalizions of Enlightenment: The Secret to the Pain (in stores now)
by Éric L Farrell

"*This book of inspirational and motivational poetry takes you through a process of healing by allowing you to follow the author through his. You will relate to his feelings and problems. While Seeking Solace deals with tragedies, Verbalizions deals more with everyday problems and struggles. Offering no apology for the Truth, Farrell wastes very little time diagnosing problems, and getting straight to the point of the solution. It's not about poetry; he addresses serious issues with serious advice on how to deal with life, and more importantly, how not to deal with life.*"

--Emaculate Publishing

ISBN: 1-931855-24-2 - trade paperback - 80 pages

"...soul-stirring stories and powerful messages showcased in a poetry written to convey a process of healing from the stresses and abuses that life inevitably imposes upon most of us." **--THE MIDWEST BOOK REVIEW**

"This book is what the world needs now! It depicts views from a true Christian perspective. I like the way Mr. Farrell connects his words to bring out his perspective of the issues we deal with daily. Yet, he boldly gives Verbalizions of Enlightenment to truly evoke thoughts. This book is a must!"

--April Barrett, poet & author
A Bright Silver Lining for those Dark Cloudy Blues

"...I was hooked from the first poem, *"Verbalizions."* I immediately felt his individual soul and uniqueness of expression. It was not hard to see why a poem written by him could emerge as the top pick of many poems submitted to the *Russell Simmons' Def Poetry Jam.*

--Sonstar Carlisle Peterson, apostle and author

book excerpt:
"Sometimes it seems like I'm just confused... constantly given two paths to choose. One on which I'll win and one on which I'll lose. I do realize that losing is a part of life, and so is learning, and so is heartache, and so is also strife..." *from... "Talking For My Health"*

About The Authors

About E&W Collaborations

Éric L Farrell & Will Holmes Jr.

As God would have it, Holmes' passion for leadership began to rub off on Farrell, as Farrell's passion for poetry began to rub off on Holmes. Both seeking to follow the same path of righteousness through Christ, E&W Collaborations inevitably began to form.

E&W Collaborations was founded by Éric & Will as **an online ministry of poetry** in **September of 1999**. Their mission was simple: to send their original inspirational poems as e-mail forwards for free. They soon included scripture and short vocabulary lists of uncommon words and Christian jargon. Occasionally, readers would reply with questions about life or simply to share their lives with Éric and Will. Four years later, E&W is still sending out their poems by e-mail with the encouragement of their readers. However, they're now venturing out to your local bookstores, churches, and poetry venues. To subscribe to E&W's monthly poem by e-mail, visit their website below.

Éric & Will share their poems with you, and leave it up to you to share them with others. This reflects their motto, "We bring it real real. We bring it real true. God-inspired writers, with a message spread by you."

E&W Collaborations' purpose is briefly stated by saying, "We're just two brothers here, trying to spread a message with a positive purpose and a spiritual essence. The lessons learned here are motivation for change, and our mission statement is to 'break the chains.'"

"Jesus is Lord" -E&W

BOOKS:
Seeking Solace*: Finding Peace and Comfort In Times of Distress*

Website: www.ewcollaborations.com

E&W: 1999 - 2003

E&W Collabo,
That's Éric, Will, and the poems
Since Fall '97 when VUU's Huntley Hall became our home.
Two friends became a poetic team,
In September '99 we had the vision,
And started the foundation for the dream.

Placed together as roommates,
And even placed in the same English class,
Allowing us to develop a bond of friendship,
And the chance to write between the assigned work of business and math.
God gave us a gift and put us together,
So we used our poetry to guide His people through stormy weather.

We kept getting mass email forwards and spam,
Chain letters and porn sites,
Coming quicker than we could hit the delete key with one hand.
All this garbage and negativity, but we had a better plan.
We'd pump positivity through email,
And send some forwards ourselves,
Every two weeks, a poem for your mental and spiritual health.

The email was free,
But for the book,
There's a necessary fee.
But we're not in it for the profits,
We're just taking that next step,
To where God wants us to be.

And we believe He will use this book,
To help the spiritually blind to see.
And use it to comfort the hearts of those,
That have found it hard to live stress and worry free.

Prayerfully and hopefully,
Seeking Solace will just be the start,
And Lord willing,
This dynamic duo will never part.

8/28/03
-Will Holmes Jr.

About the Author - Holmes

Will Holmes Jr. - born May 7, 1979 in Trenton, New Jersey to William B. Holmes, Sr. and Helen Vereen Holmes, was raised in the company of three older siblings. With a B.S. degree in Mathematics from *Virginia Union University*, Holmes was very involved in school as the *President of the* **National Society of Black Engineers (NSBE)** and Chairman of the *Student Action Committee*. He is a born and bred leader, to say the least.

Having performed at several talent shows, poetry readings, and special events at schools and clubs during his college years, Holmes is pretty familiar with the poetry scene. Holmes' poetry began as rap, which transformed into spoken word and written poetry by the second half of his freshman year. "The biggest influence in getting me into poetry, was probably my college roommate and poetical partner, Éric L Farrell," says Holmes. Placed as roommates by the university, the two were soon frequenting talent shows and events in the **Richmond VA** area; Will on rap and Éric on poetry.

After writing a few poems, Will soon realized that he could bring forth a better message through poetry. And with the compliments and positive reactions of friends and audiences, it could not be denied that Mr. Holmes had true poetic talent. Untaught, it soon became obvious that what Mr. Holmes had, was a gift. And once he found out that his poetic skill was a gift, "I knew I had to use it to help glorify God and try to influence people in the right way," he says. His inspiration for writing comes from his personal experiences, thoughts, and feelings.

Be it known, that with every poem, he seeks to convey a positive message, and express his feelings and emotions. He aims to reach hearts, and rarely does he miss his mark. "Even if only one person out of a hundred feels the true message being delivered or is comforted by the words, then that is enough for me... God is #1 in my life, because without Him, I would be nothing and would have nothing. My desire is for everyone to be able to experience God's love as I have." Holmes is currently a Systems Analyst for the Information Services Division of **Merck & Co.** Headquarters in **New Jersey.**

BOOKS:
Seeking Solace: *Finding Peace and Comfort in Times of Distress*

Website: www.willholmesjr.com

...continued from   p. 126

About the Author – Farrell

One of Farrell's greatest accomplishments is the success of his first book of inspirational poetry, *Verbalizions of Enlightenment: The Secret to the Pain*. This book has been loved by people of all ages and types. When asked to write about something influential that had changed their views, one college student chose to write about one of the included poems, "The Train," and how it changed his view of poetry. Another student preached a sermon based on this same poem from Éric's book. "That makes me feel like I'm here for a purpose."

Most people assumed that Farrell majored in English, but he felt that learning about poetry in his beginning stages would conventionalize his unorthodoxed style of writing and make him less unique. He gives all credit for his talents and successes in life to the Lord and Saviour, Jesus Christ. Farrell says, "reading the Bible has given me a deeper understanding of all areas in life and a better understanding of myself, others, and God. God speaks to us personally through the Bible. Without Him I'd be lost."

BOOKS:
Seeking Solace: Finding Peace and Comfort in Times of Distress
Verbalizions of Enlightenment: The Secret to the Pain

Website: www.ericlfarrell.com

About the Author – Farrell

photo by Elizabeth Parker

Éric L Farrell - winner of Russell Simmons' *Def Poetry Jam*, currently resides in *Woodbridge, Virginia* upon completion of this second book. His first book, **Verbalizions of Enlightenment: The Secret to the Pain**, was released in major bookstores Nationally on February 1st of 2002. With this book, the author was successful in defying all demographic barriers and reaching the hearts of people of all ages, races and creeds.

A Summa Cum Laude graduate of **Virginia Union University**, Farrell was first acknowledged for his gift of writing at the age of seven with a Write-A-Thon Author's Award, followed by a first place award the next year in the school writing competition for his short book about eating healthy. After years of scribbling rap lyrics and short tales, Farrell's knack for writing reemerged upon composing his first poem in English class in 1995 (**Woodbridge Senior High School**). When given the writing assignment, he recalls thinking, "This will be easy, I'll just write as if I'm writing rap lyrics." This worked well with him, as he has continued to write. The major influences on his writing are God, music, fellow poets, and life experiences. As a former college peer counselor he says, "To influence just one person in a positive way is a great accomplishment." Through his poetry, he is able to do this as the co-founding poet of **E&W Collaborations**, a Christian ministry of poetry - co-founded by Will Holmes Jr.

He began reading his poetry in schools, church, talent shows and poetry readings. Since, he has presented everywhere from the poetry clubs in DC and New York's acclaimed **Nuyorican Poet's Café**, all the way to the pulpits of **Nairobi, Kenya** and **Naples, Italy**. Farrell has even been the featured guest on **live talkshow TV**.

In 2001, Farrell was chosen as the *September* **Winner** of **Russell Simmons' Def Poetry Jam** (now a hit series on **HBO**) for a poem entitled *"They Follow You Follow Them"* wherein he spoke to spiritual leaders who flirt with hypocrisy and warned of the negative effects of such behavior. This poem was especially relevant during September 2001's flooded church attendance due to 9-11 tragedies. Currently, he is the Host of **WordStage Poetry Lounge** in **Richmond, VA** (sponsored in part by Barnes & Noble) and **Washington, DC,** and **WordStage Poetry TOUR.** Courtesy of Emaculate Publishing, Farrell appears on the recent CD release, **"Fearless"** (EP) by Gospel hip hop artist, **Rory Lyon** of Wordlyf.

...continued on page 125

Emaculate Publishing

~Your Guidance Counselor~

Our mission

is to enrich the mind, body, & spirit by providing Truth, enlightenment, and inspiration, while promoting self-awareness. We focus on providing guidance in all areas of life and helping people to realize their true purpose as individuals. Our underlying purpose is to manifest the power of spoken and written word and cultivate this art of expression as medicine for the soul.

Quick Order Form

Usually ships in **2-4 days**
Orders **Payable to:** Emaculate Publishing
Toll Free phone orders: 1-888-Bookway
WebSite orders: www.emaculatepublishing.com
Postal Orders, payable to: *Emaculate Publishing*/ Attn: Orders
       PO Box 1074/ Woodbridge, VA 22195-1074. USA.

Please send the following book(s):

___ (qty.) of __ Seeking Solace: In a Time of Distress (hardback) __ ($19.95/ea.)
___ (qty.) of __ Seeking Solace: In a Time of Distress (paperback) __ ($14.95/ea.)
___ (qty.) of Verbalizions of Enlightenment: The Secret to the Pain __ ($14.95/ea.)

I have requested a total of _____ (total quantity)books.
(if unsatisfied, books may be returned for a full refund, unless unsaleable.)

Name: _____
Address: _____
City:_____ State:____ Zip:_____
Telephone:_____
email address: _____

Please keep me updated about:
  ☐ Other Books/Products and Speaking/Signing Events

Shipping Charges:
U.S.: $3.95 for the first book, $1 each additional book.
International: $6.95 for the first book, $1.25 each additional book.

Payment type: ☐Check ☐ Money Order ☐ *Credit Card:*
       ☐ *Visa* ☐ *MasterCard* ☐ *Discover* ☐ *American Express*

Credit Card number:_____security digits_____
Name on card:_____Exp. date:_____

Total Books Cost + Shipping = Subtotal + (Sales tax) = Total Sale
_____ + _____ = $_____ + (_____) = $_____

(**Sales tax**: Please add 4.5% of Subtotal for products shipped to Virginia addresses.)